GOD IN STREET CLOTHES

GOD IN STREET CLOTHES

REV. DR. MELVIN VON WADE, SR.

Urban Publishing House LLC

Contents

Dedication   vii

1   "I AM the Bread of Life"   1
2   "I AM the Light of the World"   10
3   "I AM the Door"   26
4   "I AM the Good Shepherd"   38
5   "I AM the Resurrection and the Life"   48
6   "I AM the Way, the Truth, and the Life"   62
7   "I AM the True Vine"   78

Copyright ©2024 by Melvin Von Wade, Sr.

All rights reserved by the author. No part of this publication may be reproduced, stored, or transmitted in any form or by any means, electronic, mechanical, photocopying, recording, scanning, or without written permission from the author and the publisher. It is illegal to copy this book, post it to a website, or distribute it by any other means without permission from the author.

Melvin Von Wade, Sr. asserts the moral right to be identified as the author of this work.

Melvin Von Wade, Sr. has no responsibility for the persistence or accuracy of URLs for external or third-party Internet Websites referred to in this publication and does not guarantee that any content on such Websites is, or will remain, accurate or appropriate.

Legacy Hardback Edition - 979-8-8693-4857-9
Paperback Edition - 979-8-3302-9923-2
EBook - Only Available at www.urbanpublishinghouse.com/bookstore

First Published by Urban Publishing House, LLC, 2024

Camellia P. Wade McKinley (Content Editor and Proofreader)
Derrick I. Temple, Sr. (General and Line-Copy Editor, Format, Cover Design)

"Authors Who Write with Integrity, Intelligence, and Inspiration!"
P. O. Box 742
Oxnard, CA 93032
Email: admin@urbanpublishinghouse.com
Web: www.urbanpublishinghouse.com
Phone: 1-888-671-2922

Dedication

I dedicate this sermonic work to the late Rev. Dr. Gardner C. Taylor, who I came to know quite well. I refer to preachers such as Dr. Gardner C. Taylor as the preaching prototypes of the Black preaching heritage who had a keen usage of what we called, "sanctified imagination" in their sermons. This work is a series of sermons I preached in relation to the "I AM" sayings of Christ. To identify with sinful mankind, Jesus "came down" in the likeness of Man to save all humanity. Jesus would often utilize the known elements of His days on Earth to teach of Himself. They knew about bread. They needed it every day. To expand their understanding of Jesus, He would say things like, "I AM the Bread of Life." When I think of Jesus' incarnational methods of identification, I deemed no title more befitting than when Dr. Taylor would often refer to Jesus as, "God in Street Clothes."

I

"I AM the Bread of Life"

John 6:35 (KJV) - *³⁵ And Jesus said unto them, "I am the bread of life: he that cometh to me shall never hunger; and he that believeth on me shall never thirst."*

Hand in hand with the feeding of the 5,000 came a crisis. The crisis came because Jesus openly assaulted the people for their blindness and their failure to comprehend the real significance of the meal. Jesus recognized that the remnant of that five thousand who sought Him in the synagogue in Capernaum did not take cognizance of the sign that the meal signified. He knows that those who stuffed themselves the day before in the wilderness were coming to Him because it was feedtime again.

They came because of temporal benefits. He suggests that they were so dim-sighted that they could not see that God's grace enabled a crowd to be fed. Further, He suggests that their thoughts had been nailed to the things of this life. Moreover, He is suggesting that their eyes had never lifted beyond the ramparts of this world to the horizons of eternities beyond.

Jesus rebuked them for their earthbound point of view. They could not think about their souls for thinking about their stomachs. He knew they wanted bread without toil. Instead of them turning their thoughts to thinking about God, they were thinking about bread. They received bread and thought of it as bread and not as a gift of God. They exemplified, beyond a shadow of a doubt, that they were only interested in the by-products of religion. I'm sure that in the mind of Jesus, He knew that these people had come again for a manifestation of power but were in no wise concerned about interpretation.

A closer look reveals that Jesus had two groups with Him: (1) Those who were false disciples who eventually reacted in unbelief, and (2) those who were true disciples who acted in belief. The false disciples were attracted to the physical phenomena. Jesus seeking to expose the shallowness of the false disciples and their pretension, says in a word of command, "Don't work for the food which perishes, work for the food which lasts forever and which gives eternal life."

Jesus wanted them to know that there are far bigger and more satisfying things within our reach than bread. Jesus' whole point was that all these Jews were interested in was physical satisfaction. They had received an unexpected free and lavish meal. Their bellies were full yesterday, and they had returned today for another output. But Jesus wanted them to be aware that there are two kinds of hunge. There is a physical hunger that physical food can satisfy, but there is a hunger more paramount than physical hunger; there is a spiritual hunger. Physical, material food can in no wise satisfy spiritual hunger. A man can be stuffed with mundane, earthly bread and yet experience this haunting dissatisfaction; this unsatisfied longing within his heart, and incompleteness within his life. At the same time, we can be appallingly full and appallingly hungry. St. Augustine said, "Thou has made us for thyself, and our souls are restless until we find rest in thee."

When Jesus finishes rebuking the crowd for their purely materialistic notions, He tells them "Not to labor for food which perishes, but for food which endures to everlasting life." When Jesus had finished His command about laboring for food which endures to everlasting life, the Jews immediately began to think in terms of doing good works. It was

1

"I AM the Bread of Life"

John 6:35 (KJV) - *35 And Jesus said unto them, "I am the bread of life: he that cometh to me shall never hunger; and he that believeth on me shall never thirst."*

Hand in hand with the feeding of the 5,000 came a crisis. The crisis came because Jesus openly assaulted the people for their blindness and their failure to comprehend the real significance of the meal. Jesus recognized that the remnant of that five thousand who sought Him in the synagogue in Capernaum did not take cognizance of the sign that the meal signified. He knows that those who stuffed themselves the day before in the wilderness were coming to Him because it was feedtime again.

They came because of temporal benefits. He suggests that they were so dim-sighted that they could not see that God's grace enabled a crowd to be fed. Further, He suggests that their thoughts had been nailed to the things of this life. Moreover, He is suggesting that their eyes had never lifted beyond the ramparts of this world to the horizons of eternities beyond.

Jesus rebuked them for their earthbound point of view. They could not think about their souls for thinking about their stomachs. He knew they wanted bread without toil. Instead of them turning their thoughts to thinking about God, they were thinking about bread. They received bread and thought of it as bread and not as a gift of God. They exemplified, beyond a shadow of a doubt, that they were only interested in the by-products of religion. I'm sure that in the mind of Jesus, He knew that these people had come again for a manifestation of power but were in no wise concerned about interpretation.

A closer look reveals that Jesus had two groups with Him: (1) Those who were false disciples who eventually reacted in unbelief, and (2) those who were true disciples who acted in belief. The false disciples were attracted to the physical phenomena. Jesus seeking to expose the shallowness of the false disciples and their pretension, says in a word of command, "Don't work for the food which perishes, work for the food which lasts forever and which gives eternal life."

Jesus wanted them to know that there are far bigger and more satisfying things within our reach than bread. Jesus' whole point was that all these Jews were interested in was physical satisfaction. They had received an unexpected free and lavish meal. Their bellies were full yesterday, and they had returned today for another output. But Jesus wanted them to be aware that there are two kinds of hunge. There is a physical hunger that physical food can satisfy, but there is a hunger more paramount than physical hunger; there is a spiritual hunger. Physical, material food can in no wise satisfy spiritual hunger. A man can be stuffed with mundane, earthly bread and yet experience this haunting dissatisfaction; this unsatisfied longing within his heart, and incompleteness within his life. At the same time, we can be appallingly full and appallingly hungry. St. Augustine said, "Thou has made us for thyself, and our souls are restless until we find rest in thee."

When Jesus finishes rebuking the crowd for their purely materialistic notions, He tells them "Not to labor for food which perishes, but for food which endures to everlasting life." When Jesus had finished His command about laboring for food which endures to everlasting life, the Jews immediately began to think in terms of doing good works. It was always a Jewish conviction that by living a good and moral life, a man could win and earn the favor of God.

The Jews asked Jesus what the work of God was. They expected Jesus to lay down some rules and regulations and a list of things that they must do, but that is not what Jesus said at all. The answer of Jesus was extremely compressed. Jesus reminded them to believe in Him who God hath sent. They responded by saying, "Very well, prove it." Jesus then reminds them that it was not Moses who had given them the manna, it was God. Secondly, He told them that the manna was not really the bread of God, it was only the symbol of the bread of God. Jesus said that the bread of God is He who comes down from Heaven and gives men life, not simply assuaging or satisfaction from physical hunger. Jesus claimed that it is Christ alone who can satisfy the immortal longings and the insatiable hunger of the spirit and soul.

Finally, Jesus plainly makes the first of His seven great, "I AM" claims in John. He says, "I AM the Bread of Life!" But Jesus did not stop there. Jesus identified this bread of life with His own body and blood, which He said men must eat in order to enter into life, which is life indeed, and which death cannot touch.

Now, to understand the roots of this statement, go back to the Old Testament. Any mentioning of bread from Heaven immediately turned the thoughts of a Jew to Exodus 16 in the Wilderness of Sin where God gave them manna in their wilderness journeyings. That was even deeply imprinted in the minds of the Jews. To the Jews, there was something mysteriously divine about manna, which literally means, "What is it?" In Nehemiah 9, this manna is called, "bread from Heaven." In Psalm 78:24, it is called, "the corn of Heaven." And in Psalm 78:25, manna was said to be angels' food.

On the other hand, Jesus is also careful to stress the fact that their statement about Moses being the giver of the manna was inaccurate. Moses did not give bread from Heaven. The truth is that Moses prayed, and God gave the manna from Heaven. Jesus was cognizant of the fact that it was a standard part of Jewish belief that the manna was given because of the transcendent merits of Moses. Jesus however, corrected that and insisted that the giver of the manna was not a human person, but God. And it was not given on the merit of Moses, but it was given by the mercy of God.

The Jews bitterly resented Him saying, "I AM the Bread of Life." They felt He had no right, for they knew Him. They rejected Jesus because they tested Him by human assessments, by social values, and by worldly standards. By rejecting this Galilean carpenter, they disregarded God's greatest miracle and message.

The Jews were enraged because they caught the implications. For Jesus to say that He was The Bread of Life was to say that He was the Messiah, and that with Him came the messianic age. For it was a part of Jewish messianic beliefs that when the Messiah would come, He would once again feed His people with Heavenly manna. It was the belief of the Rabbis that the Messiah would be a second Moses. Hence, whatever Moses did, the Messiah would duplicate. For Jesus to insist that God gives the Living Bread and that He is the Living Bread, is to claim that He is nothing less than Deity.

Finding these words difficult and puzzling, and being attracted by His miracles but not His message, the crowd angrily became religious drop-outs for they went back and walked no more with Him. Jesus then turned to His disciples, and asked them, "Would ye also go away?" Peter simply, but sublimely replies, "Lord, we don't pretend to understand you, but we have seen too much to desert you. We believe in you, however puzzled we may be over what you say. We have seen God in you as we have not seen in no one else. You have the words of eternal life. We cannot find them anywhere else. We won't leave you, for there is nowhere else to go."

What is the meaning of this self-affirmation, "I AM the Bread of Life?" Do you suppose that Jesus is inviting us to engage ourselves in some cannibalistic orgy? No. We must be forever aware that Jesus was always using some physical terms to express some spiritual truths. Consequently, we must always seek to look behind the physical symbol in order to get the spiritual meaning. If we fail to do this, then we will never know the true meaning of His words. Jesus was not suggesting cannibalism. He was only describing the intimate relationship between He and those who believe in Him.

I. The Necessity of Bread – Verses 53-58

Bread is not a luxury – bread is necessary to the life of the body. We must have bread appropriate to our bodies if we are to live. It is bread that sustains and gives nourishment to life. We must depend upon bread for our essential existence. Bread is one of the three essentials that we must have to live. The other two are air and water. We can only go 40 days without bread. Bread is the staff of life. Bread enables life to go on.

Jesus was by no means blind to the necessity of bread. And to prove it, Jesus told us to pray for bread. Jesus said, "Give us this day our daily bread." Here Jesus is acknowledging man's need for bread. Jesus is saying, don't ask for bread in a metaphorical sense, but ask as that which is a requirement for daily sustenance. Scholars say that request is in the progressive tense, which means to ask Him and keep on asking for daily bread. Jesus seems to suggest that just as one's physical perishing life depends on bread, your spiritual everlasting life depends upon the Bread of Life. And Jesus is the Bread of Life. Spiritual life depends upon Him.

One of the great tragedies of this life is that too many people are trying to live this life without the presence of the necessary Jesus. They are in ignorance of the *essentialness* of Jesus. Because they don't know that He is the ultimate, indispensable, they seek to live their lives without Him. They have the false illusion that life can be lived independently of Jesus and still be meaningful and purposeful.

It's sad that people are trying to live without Jesus. What really warps our thinking is the fact that many seem to do well in this life without Jesus. There are many who have money, power, prestige, social standing, houses, land, jobs, family, and no Jesus! It is a fact that you can exist without Jesus. You can have an *ontologically-active* existence without Jesus. But to live life with a selfish disregard for Jesus is really to live life backwards. And if you look at the word, "live," you see that "live" spelled backwards is "evil." It's evil to seek to live without Jesus.

But I want to tell us that we can occur and exist without Jesus, but we can't survive in this life without Jesus. We may manage for a while, but we are going to need Jesus one day. And it is sad that so many have to be driven to the point that it is clear that they need Jesus. The Lord knows how to orchestrate and navigate situations and circumstances in our lives to prove to us that we need Him. I don't want Him to send me a designated disaster to show me that I need Him; I know I need Him. Like bread, Jesus is necessary.

II. The Provider of Bread – Verses 38-40

That which is so essential and necessary is provided by the providential God. Just like physical bread is God-given, so is the spiritual bread divinely provided. Just like God gives grain, so God hath given His Son. Just like God sends the rain and sunshine, so hath God sent His Son. Don't you hear Jesus saying in verse 38, "For I came down from Heaven, not to do mine own will, but the will of Him that sent me." The central theme of Scripture is God giving, God providing, and God sending His Son.

Salvation hinges on the fact that God sent and God gave His Son. Redemption centers around the fact that God sent and God gave His Son. We are justified because God sent and God gave His Son. Our deliverance from eternal burn is based upon the fact that God sent and God gave His Son. Again and again, in the Scripture, we see where the essential Jesus has been sent by the Great Sender. Isaiah 9:6 reads, "Unto us, a child is born. Unto us a Son is given: and the government shall be upon His shoulders: and His name shall be called Wonderful, Counselor, the Mighty God, the Everlasting Father, the Prince of Peace."

The latter portion of Isaiah 61:1 says, "He hath sent me to bind up the brokenhearted, to proclaim liberty to the captives, and the opening of the prison to them that are bound, to proclaim the acceptable year of the Lord." In John 3:16-17 we read, "For God so loved the world, that He gave His only Begotten Son, that whosoever believeth in Him should not perish, but have everlasting life. For God sent not His Son into the world to condemn the world; but that the world through Him might be saved that sent me."

In John 9:4, He said, "I must work the works of Him that sent me, while it is day: the night cometh, when no man can work." In John 20:21, Jesus says, "As my Father hath sent me, even so send I you." In Galatians 4:4-5, Paul says, "But when the fullness of time was come, God sent forth His Son, made of a woman, made under the law, to redeem them that were under the law, that we might receive the adoption of sons."

God sending Jesus is purposeful sending. Just like God-sent bread is tied to life, the God-sent Bread of Life is tied to life. Jesus said, "I come that they might have life and that they might have it more abundantly." In the Text, Jesus says, "I AM the living bread which came down from Heaven: if any man eat of this bread, he shall live forever." God sent Jesus for life purposes. What Jesus does is, He equates belief to intake. Intake is as necessary spiritually as it is physically. Anybody who intakes or believes that Jesus was sent by God has life.

I think I ought to tell you that I had a spiritual intake of Jesus. I believed God sent Jesus for life purposes. Because I believed, everything changed. Old things passed away, and all things become brand new.

III. Bread Is Satisfying

In verse 35, Jesus says, "I AM the Bread of Life, he that cometh to me shall never hunger; and he that believeth on me shall never thirst." Hunger is a most demanding physical need. There is a part of Man that only bread can satisfy. Jesus knew this, but the Devil knew it too. Therefore, the Devil tried to ensnare and entrap Jesus along this line. If you can recall Jesus' temptation experience, you will recall the Devil telling Jesus that there was a side of Man that had an insatiable appetite, and only bread could satisfy that longing. Therefore, the Devil said to Jesus, "Give men bread and, men will follow you; they will serve you, and ultimately you will win the world."

Because of the fact that Man sees more than he hears, and because Man will be more attracted to what they do rather than who they are, please them and they will follow you. I've noticed that hunger is of such a nature that hunger affects your total being. When you are hungry, it affects not only your stomach, but it also affects your nerves, your mind, your head, your strength, your hands, and your legs.

When you appropriate bread to the body, it satisfies your total physical being. That's what Jesus does. There is a side of Man that only Jesus can satisfy. Man is more than a material animal. Man is a spiritual being. Therefore, He must have something deeper than ephemeral, temporary, or transient things.

A fatal tragedy is that many men see themselves as a dichotomy. Therefore, they seek to satisfy their mind and body. They satisfy their stomachs with food. They satisfy their eyes with light. They satisfy their ears with sound. They satisfy their lungs with air. They satisfy their minds with knowledge. But men ignore the fact that Man is a trichotomous and not a dichotomy. Man is mind, body, and soul or spirit.

As a result, the soul or spirit of Man is made to feast on indigestible jewels. When you try to feed your soul or spirit on things of this world, it rejects them and starves. There is bread that is adapted for man's spiritual nature. Jesus knows it. That's why He said, "I AM the Bread of Life." Then your soul or spirit knows it. Don't you hear your soul crying out, "Bread of Heaven, Bread of Heaven, feed me til I want no more." This Bread of Heaven will satisfy a hungry soul. David said, "O taste and see that the Lord is good." In order to see how satisfying He is, the only way you can taste and see that the Lord is good, you have to have an intake of His Word. David said, "Thy word have I hid in my heart that I might not sin against thee."

It nourishes – It teaches – It ignites – It enlightens – It convinces – It informs –It convicts – It entreats –It converts – It enriches – It counsels – It guides – It abides – It leads – It restrains – It constrains – It abstains – It refrains – It entertains – It sustains – It maintains – It stimulates – It exhilarates – It captivates – It exonerates – It renovates

– It castigates – It restorates – It separates – It activates – It generates – It dedicates – It consecrates – It motivates – It invigorates It energizes – It spiritualizes – It revives It electrifies – It justifies – It dignifies – It purifies – It clarifies – It classifies – It beautifies – It sanctifies.

By doing all of this, it satisfies my soul. And f you want to find out how satisfying the Lord is, get the Word of the Lord, and still away, and read it.

2

"I AM the Light of the World"

John 8:12 (KJV) - *¹² Then spake Jesus again unto them, saying, "I am the light of the world: he that followeth me shall not walk in darkness, but shall have the light of life."*

Jesus was a master at taking advantage of opportunities. Because of His unique awareness, and prolific insight, He could take the *most simple* and make it *most sublime*. He seemed forever ready to express a cosmic truth. He always seemed to look for ways and means of transmitting messages for the sake of the Kingdom. Jesus made everything count: He made little children, foot-washing, a little lad's lunch, sickness, death, rejection, a request for water at a wedding. reprimands from critics, and even traps...He made them all count. He used all of these avenues and more, for the sake of His Kingdom.

Another thing to note is the fact that Jesus came to Earth to redeem Man with a dual priority. But because God, unlike the mysterious unknowable gods of other religions, is a self-revealing God, Jesus' other priority was to reveal to Man what God is like. This axiom shows us that Jesus' preaching far excels man's preaching, for we exegete the text, but Jesus exegeted God. And, in exegeting God to the commonplace where we can understand, Jesus, takes the commonplace in order to expose Man to the real truths about God. So, what He does is, He takes and uses the ordinary in order to speak of the extraordinary. He uses the physical to speak of the spiritual. He uses the temporal to speak of the eternal. He uses the earthly to speak of the heavenly. He uses the terrestrial to speak of the celestial. He uses the limited to speak of the unlimited. He uses the finite to speak of the infinite. He uses the transparent to reveal the opaque. He uses the *here and now* to speak of the *hereafter*. That's why Jesus is God incarnate. That's why He is the Word made flesh. And our text is another graphic example of how Jesus takes the mundane and uses it to express a divine transcendent truth.

In order to understand this text, I deem it necessary that we examine where Jesus was when He made this self affirmation claim. Jesus makes this claim in what is known as the Temple Treasury. The Temple Treasury was in what is known as the Court of the Women, which was the second of the Temple courts. The Court of the Women was so called because women could not pass beyond this point unless they were actually going to offer a sacrifice on the altar which was in the Court of the Priests.

Around the Court of the Women was a colonnade or a porch. In that porch, against the wall were thirteen treasure chests. Those treasure chests were called, "The Trumpets." The people were to drop their offerings into these trumpets.

The Temple Treasury was a busy place, for there was always a constant flow of people coming and going, placing their money in some of the treasures. So, there would be no better place to collect an audience of devout people than at the Temple Treasury.

Secondly, I think it is quite significant when He made this claim. The place is significant, but the season is also significant. It is late Autumn, the barley, the wheat and the grape harvest had been safely in-gathered. So, late Autumn means that it is Feast of the Tabernacle time. This feast was to commemorate the journeys through the wilderness by the people of Israel. This occasion was also called, "The Festival of Booths" because throughout its seven-day celebration, people left their houses and lived in little booths or tabernacles. These booths were temporary structures (made of branches and leaves from palm trees). These booths were to be constructed in such a way that one would have protection from inclement weather but so as never to shut out the sun. The roof had to be thatched or covered, but it was to be covered in such a way that the stars could be visibly seen at night.

The historical significance of this was to remind the people that there was a time when they had been homeless wanderers in the desert without a roof over their heads before they entered the Promised Land. Originally, this feast lasted for seven days, but by the time of Jesus, the feast lasted for eight days. This festival was one of the three festivals in which it was compulsory for every adult Jewish male who lived within a twenty-mile radius of Jerusalem to attend.

At the end the first day of the Feast of the Tabernacle, a most dramatic and notable ceremony took place. When evening was come, the Court of the Women was filled to capacity. When darkness had come, four young priest would climb the ladder. And upon receiving a given signal, each young priest would light a wick in a gigantic candelabra which was placed in a golden bowl and was filled with oil. The light from those four candelabras was so great until it was said to have illuminated every street, every court, and every square in Jerusalem. The blaze from the candelabras reminded the people of the light which had guided them in their pilgrim days.

Jewish historians tell us that Jesus' voice rang out at the Temple Treasury saying "I AM the Light of the World. He who follows me will not walk in darkness." In saying, "I AM the Light of the World," Jesus again inks Himself to Eternal Deity, because in Jewish thought and language, Yahweh was especially associated with light. Job 29.3 says. "By His light I walked through darkness." Psalm 36:9 says, "In thy light, shall we see light." Psalm 104:1-2 says, "O Lord my God, Thou art very great, thou art clothed with honor and majesty who coverest Thyself with light as with a garment." Isaiah 60:20 says, "The Lord shall be thine Everlasting Light." Daniel 2:22 tells us that "the light dwelleth with Him." Habakkuk 3:4 says, "His brightness was as the light." In Zechariah 14:5-8, the emphasis is upon God as the Light of the World who gives living water to His people. The Old Testament closes with Malachi saying, "the sun of righteousness would arise with heating in His wings."

And then, in the New Testament, we are told that light is one of the three limited definitions of God. In John 4:24, we are told that "God is Spirit." In 1 John 4.8, we are told that "God is Love." And finally, in 1 John 1:5, it says, "God is Light." Now these expressions relate to the very inherent nature of God, and they tell us in limited fashion what God is, in and of Himself.

So, when Jesus says, "I AM the Light of the World," Jesus is announcing the fact that He is Absolutely Deity. The theologians would say that Jesus is "homoousios" with the Father. And what that means is that Jesus is the same in substance as the Father. He is co-equal, co-eternal, co existent, and co-essential with the Father. He is the exact likeness of the Father. He is the accurate expression of God's person and glory. He is one (who is) eternally present with the Father. He is *God of very God*, And He is God's *un-begun* and unending reflection of Himself.

In other words, based upon John 1:14, Jesus is God in Street Clothes.

But now, when Jesus used the incommunicable name "I AM," and laid claim on the fact that He is Deity and equated Himself with God the Father, and pronounced Himself as the looked-for Messiah, it was met with utter rejection. Jesus said that they rejected Him because they judged after the flesh. They rejected His self-affirmation because of familiarity. Familiarity breeds contempt, and closeness dwarfs greatness. And here, Jesus' claim to deity and messiahship is denounced because people were too close. They were acquainted with His background. They knew His mother, His foster father, His brothers, and sisters. They even knew that He came from Nazareth. And they saw no connection between familiarity peasantry, obscurity, and deity. In essence, how could one who would dare confess that "The birds have nests, foxes have holes, but I have nowhere to lay my head, be God." But in spite of their rejection and disbelief, Jesus says, "I AM the Light of t the world."

When you look at the text, you will notice that Jesus says, He and darkness are mutually exclusive. In other words, if there is Jesus, there is no darkness. And if there is darkness, there is an absence of Jesus. For Jesus is the antithesis to darkness. You see, darkness is diametrically opposite of Jesus. In the Bible, light is a symbol of deity, but in contrast, darkness is a symbol for sin, ignorance, guilt, depravity, and misery. And Satan is the author and father of darkness. And since Jesus is represented by light, and darkness represents Satan and sin, and by them being mutually repellent, it is impossible for them to co-exist. There is indisputable evidence that Jesus is conspicuously missing.

I have come to realize that we don't want to own up to the fact that it is dark in this world. And, the reason that we don't want to own up to this darkness is because we have made the grave mistake of equating intelligent enlightenment and mental discernment, scholarly erudition, and philosophical intellectuality, with light.

The world is forever talking about "enlightenment." Since the renaissance of the fifteenth and sixteenth century, when man began to take a new interest in knowledge, one of man's favorite words has been "enlightenment." This rebirth in learning and knowledge marked a great turning point in history. A similar revival occurred in the eighteenth century. This period became known as "The Age of Enlightenment." Knowledge, they say, is that which brings light.

But I stand to say, that though there has been an increase in knowledge; though our knowledge has increased in a technological and a scientific sense; though we have discovered great and new knowledge; though our knowledge about the processes of nature, about physical illness, diseases, and many other subjects has been phenomenal; though this new knowledge has thrown a great light upon the working of the whole cosmos, it does not matter how much enlightenment we get, wherever Christ does not rule and reign, there is an absence of light. Where there is an absence of light, there is darkness. The Bible is blunt in the assertion that we have physical life without spiritual light.

Though we may know a lot, there is an obvious absence of Christ. We may be richly educated, but we are still groping in spiritual darkness. And it goes without saying that there is an obvious absence of Christ. All we have to do is look around and we can see an absence of Christ the Light.

To prove it, we know it's dark when we see that our news headlines read hate crimes, random killing, slain hostages, covert racism, nuclear war, bio-terrorism, war based on lies, suicide bombings, dishonesty, gang violence, corruption, pollution, inflation, budget cuts, and scams. We know it's dark when we see where there is child pornography and where the main headline word is pedophilia and where small children are being abducted, abused, molested, and murdered, and when it has reached epidemic proportions, it let's you know that it's dark. There are so many missing persons, especially children, and in particular, little girls as well as women. We see now that men are promising non-American girls and women freedom in America only to find out when they arrive in America that they are not free, but they are sex slaves.

We know it's dark. In every major city, there is a skid row that is infested with pimps, prostitutes, perverts, pushers, junkies, and alcoholics. It lets you know it's dark when abortion is applauded and legalized, when sinful shacking is preferred above Godly marriage, it lets you know that it's dark when we are not interested in the divine institution of marriage, all we are concerned about is shacking, singing "The Thong Song," rocking the boat, excreting pimp juice, knocking boots, getting the swerve on, bip-bam thank you ma'am, getting laid, and hit-it-and-quit-it. That ought to tell you that it's dark. When we see where men are wanting husband's privileges with boyfriend status and men are refusing to be fathers. All they want is to be sperm donors. It's dark.

When the order of the day is alternative lifestyles, coming out of the closet, and open gay pride, and same sex marriages; when men look like women and women are looking like dudes, that says, it's dark. When homosexual men are looking for trade or chicken hawk activity in spite of the pestilence of the AIDS epidemic, it lets you know that it's dark.

When lesbian women are forever on the lookout for women who have been abused, battered, wounded, hurt, and deeply scarred, to passionately and softly comfort them, not for the purpose of healing their hurts, but in order to turn them on and out to where they will become their "cookie," you know that it's dark. When we see where people who are engaged in illicit adulterous relationships openly flaunt their sinful behavior, and tell God, in a spirit of rebellion and pride, "We shall not be bound by God's rule," it's dark.

When we see how we mirror and reflect Sodom and Gomorrah, and then see Romans 1, where it says that God gave them up to uncleanness, vile affections, and a reprobate mind, that ought to tell you, it's dark.

When we see where God's name is no longer holy, and His church is no longer sacred. When we see where those who profess Christ will say anything and do anything in the House of God, it's dark! Churches are not a place of worship and praise, but have been reduced to mere mess houses, junkyards, and garbage cans. Tension and unrest are the climate and atmosphere of the church instead of holiness, and churches are forever going to court. Because our churches are filled with noble/savages, the pastor is no longer a Christological shepherd, but a zoological zookeeper. The pastor has to spend more time putting out personality fires than he has time to do Christ-centered ministry.

Our churches are called to be contagious, arson-like incendiary fellowships. But instead, our churches have become deep freezers, our members are icebergs, our leaders are cold-storages, and our preachers are refrigerated. Our churches have become well-kept mausoleums. The church now is more stationary than missionary. Our members are proving by their muted praise that God's grace is no longer an amazing grace, but it's boring grace. That says, it's dark! But in the midst of the world's darkness, Jesus says, "I AM the Light of the World: he that followeth me shall not walk in darkness."

So, there is an absence of Jesus. Our prayer ought to be for the presence of Jesus, for the light of Jesus will dispel this world's darkness. The question is, what message is Jesus seeking to convey when He says, "I AM the Light of the World?" In order for us to understand what He means, we must interpret it in the light and context of what the Feast of the Tabernacle and what the "Pillar of Cloud" and the "Pillar of Fire" was for the Israelites in their wilderness wanderings. The "Pillar of Cloud" was for the Israelites in their wilderness wanderings. The "Pillar of Cloud" and the "Pillar of Fire" represented at least three things for the Israelites.

I. The Light Represents the Divine Director (That Is, One Who Lays Down the Rules and Sets the Direction)

The "Pillar of Cloud" was the primary means by which God guided His people from Egypt to Canaan. On their way, there were no intelligible landmarks. As a result, the cloud was the only thing that they had to keep them from wandering. Where the cloud abode, the children of Israel pitched their tents. Where the cloud tarried, the Israelites remained. And when the cloud moved, they moved. The cloud represented their guidance.

So, when Jesus claimed to be the Light of the world, He is claiming that like the "Pillar of Cloud," He is the guide for all who follow Him. We as Christians are classified as sheep. And like sheep, we don't see well. Therefore, we need guidance.

Like the Israelites journeyed from Egypt to Canaan, every believer is on a journey. Like John Bunyan says in his allegorical book, "The Pilgrim's Progress," we are en route to the Celestial City, the Paradise of God, where we still see the Tree of Life and eat it's imperishable food. There, we will see no sickness, no sorrow, no affliction, and no death. There, we shall receive comfort for all of our trials, and joy for all of our sorrows. There, we shall wear crowns of gold and enjoy the perpetual sight of the Holy One.

But now, take note of the silence that exists in the interval between Jesus' initial invitation, "Follow Me," and our ultimate arrival into that Heavenly Celestial City where we will see Him and He will say, "Well done." We know that we are en route from Earth to Heaven. We know that Earth is our point of departure, and Heaven is our point of destination. But there is silence as to the route that we shall take. Notice that Jesus does not offer us any pre-flight itineraries, no navigation systems, Map Quest, or Google Maps. He simply says, "Follow Me."

In the New Testament, there are a number of "Follow Me" passages, but none of them have specific trafficking information attached to them. In Matthew 4:19, Jesus said to Peter and Andrew, "Follow Me, and I will make you fishers of men." In Matthew 16:24, Jesus said to His disciples, "If any man will come after Me, let him deny himself, and take up his cross, and follow Me." In Matthew 19:21, Jesus said to the rich young ruler, "Go and sell that thou hast, and give to the poor, and thou shalt have treasure in Heaven: and come and follow Me." In John 1:43, Jesus saw Philip and said to him, "Follow Me." In John 10:27, Jesus said, "My sheep hear My voice, and I know them, and they follow Me."

Paul even said in 1 Corinthians 11:1, "Be ye followers of Me, even as I also am of Christ." David does tell us that He leads us in the paths of righteousness for His name's sake." But with all of these passages dealing with following Christ, specific information is missing.

Now, if we don't know the specifics of the interval between the already and the not yet, and since we are resident aliens, foreigners, and sojourners here, it behooves us to always be where the Shepherd is. He should not be in one place, while we are in another place. As sheep, not only don't we see well, but we also have the perennial inclination to wander and stray. We love to read Psalm 23 and get consolation.

However, I am here to tell us that in the midst of the comforts, compassion, and bounties of Psalm 23, there is a painful element in Psalm 23. In verse 3 it says, "He restoreth my soul." This is about when the shepherd detects a sheep whose bent is not to be close, but to wander, and stray, the shepherd personally breaks the leg of the sheep and then restores it.

And while in the mending process, he keeps the sheep close to him to teach the sheep where the sheep is supposed to be. Jesus, the shepherd, will likewise do some radical and painful stuff to us to teach us to stay close to Him.

There's a story about a shepherd who lived in Ireland. And his granddaughter went to visit him. While visiting him, she walked into a barn and saw a young lamb with its leg in a splint. She wondered what happened; she wanted to know. "Oh," said the old shepherd, "he had a bad habit of running off, so the other day, I broke his leg." When the old man told here that, she began to cry. "Why on earth would you do that", she asked. "Well," he said, "the little guy had a bad habit of running off. Every time he would do that, he would be in danger. He could fall off the edge of a cliff and kill himself, or a wolf or some other predator could find him, kill him and eat him. Every time he ran off, I would have to go find him. Then, I would set him with the rest of the flock only to have him run off again. So, I broke his leg. But that's not the end of it. After I broke his leg, I also mended it. I put a splint on it, all the while, I was talking to him, comforting him, and consoling him. Now, I have to carry water in to him every day. Not only that, I have to feed him by hand. As I do, I continue to talk to him and comfort him. By the time his leg heals, he will know my voice. He will know that it is I who takes care of him. He will come when I call him. He will stay with me, no matter what. Now, I will be able to lead him. This lamb will one day be the best sheep of the flock–Why? Because the other day, I broke his leg. In order to break its will, I had to break its leg."

Often, for God to be able to use us, He must first breaks us. Before He can use us, He must break our wills. And there comes a time when God says, "By any means necessary." Some of us have it wrong, but I'm here to tell us that God is a good shepherd.

God is more concerned about what's happening in us than He is about what's happening to us. So, as the Divine Director, He has the sovereign right to lay down the rules and set the direction. So, since He lays down the rules and sets the direction, He seeks to teach us that we don't have the right nor the freedom to be where we want to be, but we are to be where He wants us to be, and go where He wants us to go. So, our daily prayer ought to be:

Close to thee, Lord, close to Thee. All along this pilgrim journey, Saviour let me walk with Thee.

Saviour, lead me, lest I stray, gently, lead me all the way; I am safe when by thy side, I would in Thy love abide.
Thou the refuge of my soul – When life's stormy billows roll, I am safe when Thou art nigh, all my hopes on Thee rely.
Saviour, lead me, then at last, when the storm of life is past. To the land of endless day, where all tears are wiped away.
Lead me, lead me, Saviour, lead me, lest I stray. Gently down the stream of time, lead me, Saviour, all the way.

Our prayer ought to be:

Guide me o thou Great Jehovah; Pilgrim through this barren land. I am weak but thou are mighty; Hold me with thou powerful hand.

We use to sing, "Let Jesus lead you, let Jesus lead you. Let Jesus lead you, all the way. All the way from Earth to Glory. Let Jesus lead you, all the way." And I think I need to tell us that He's a mighty good leader.

II. The Light Represents Divine Dwelling and Defense

Not only did the "Pillar of Cloud" and "Pillar of Fire" suggest guidance, but it also suggested dwelling, presence, defense, and protection. When the children were on their way to Canaan, they had to deal with sweltering desert daytime heat and nighttime freezing cold. They had to deal with Pharaoh and his host seeking to overtake them. But because of God's perpetual presence and His dwelling, miraculous defense and provision, they were protected from nature's elements and worldly enemies. To further show us how miraculous His presence and protection were and how minute the details of the presence and protection were for forty years, the children of Israel walked, and their feet did not swell, and their clothes never wore out.

And like the miraculous cloud protected Israel, Jesus, our Light, is our defense and protection. I've discovered that some people have misgivings, misnomers, and false illusions about being saved. They believe that being a child of God is an easy, prosperous, healthy, and wealthy road. But I want to tell us that being a child of God is not easy. In fact, it's downright dangerous. And there are signs everywhere that seek to apprise us about this dangerous journey.

The Bible is replete with predictive suffering passages. The Psalmist said, "Many are the afflictions of the righteous." Jesus said, "In the world, ye shall have tribulation." Paul said, "We are troubled on every side." Acts 14:22 reads, "We must through much tribulation enter into the Kingdom of God." 2 Timothy 3:12 states, "All that will live godly in Christ Jesus shall suffer persecution." Peter said, "Beloved, think it not strange concerning the fiery trial which is to try you."

Somehow, we don't seem to realize that we are in a war. We sing it, but I don't think that we believe it, and that song is, "I'm on the battlefield for my Lord." And because it's warfare, its "danger time." And for the Lord's people, it's been "danger time" for a long time.

It's danger time because the Devil is trying to hinder and devour us. It's dangerous because Satan is seeking permission to sift us like wheat. It's dangerous because the natural and the supernatural have engaged in an unholy collision and are trying to separate us from the love of God. It's dangerous because we are like lambs in the midst of ravenous wolves. It's dangerous because sheep are being assaulted by a roaring lion. It's dangerous because we are like wheat choked by tares. It's dangerous because it is a war going on against foes we can't see. It's dangerous because we are being attacked by Satan, his demons, the flesh, and the world.

Paul makes it clear that it's dangerous, for he writes, "For we wrestle not against flesh and blood, but against principalities, against powers, against the rulers of the darkness of this world, against spiritual wickedness in high places." The songwriter seeks to add his addendum about our misgivings about it being an easy pathway, for he writes:

1. Am I a soldier of the cross, a follower of the lamb? And shall I fear to own His cause, or blush to speak His name?

2. Must I be carried to the skies on flow'ry beds of ease, while others fought to win the prize, and sailed through bloody seas?
3. Are there no foes for me to face? Must I not stem the flood? Is this vile world a friend to grace, to help me on to God?
4. Sure I must fight, if I would reign; increase my courage. Lord, I'll bear the toil, endure the pain, supported by Thy Word.

- Abel was murdered.
- Joseph was thrown into a pit.
- Israel was put in hard slavery.
- Moses was plotted on.
- Samson was imprisoned and blinded.
- Mordecai was sentenced to be hung.
- Job suffered satanic persecution.
- David was threatened and chased by the king and his own son.
- Zachariah the son of the priest Jehoiada was killed.
- Jeremiah was thrown in prison, and then, into a muddy cistern.
- The three Hebrews were thrown into the fiery furnace.
- Daniel was thrown into a lions' den.
- John the Baptist was beheaded.
- Jesus was crucified.
- James was hacked to death.
- Peter was crucified upside down.
- Stephen was stoned to death
- John was banished to a lonely island.
- Paul had his head chopped off on Nero's chopping clock.

Hebrews 11 says there were those who were tortured, imprisoned, stoned, scourged, sawn asunder, slain with the sword, afflicted, and tormented. In the early first century A.D., Christians were burned at the stake, and literally split apart. But in the midst of dangers, seen and unseen, Jesus, the Light of the World, has promised His presence, and He promised to protect us from all hurt, harm, and danger. Jesus said, "I will never leave thee, nor forsake thee."

There is a story about a church man who was in a hurry to get to church one night. Instead of walking the streets, he cut through the alley. While walking down the alley, a man suddenly appeared and asked him if he had a light. The church man lit the man's cigarette and rushed on to the church. The next morning while reading the paper, the church man sees the man he met in the alley on the front page of the newspaper arrested for murder. The church man told his wife that he was going down to the jail to talk to the man and find out why he would do such a thing. The church man got up and went to the jail to see the man to see if he could find out why this man had done the killing. In the midst of the conversation, the killer told the church man, "I killed him, but I really intended to kill you. The only reason that I didn't kill you was because when I asked you for a light and you lit the match, when you lit the match, I saw two men standing over your shoulder." I tell you that God in the midst of danger, will defend and protect you.

That's why David could write, "Surely goodness and mercy shall follow me all the days of my life." It's been danger time for a long time, but the Psalmist told me to tell us that in the midst of danger, turmoil, and upheaval, God is our refuge and strength, a very present help in trouble. Therefore, will not we fear. Though the Earth be removed, and though the mountains be carried into the midst of the sea. Though the waters thereof roar and be troubled, though the mountains shake with the swelling thereof, there is a river, the streams whereof shall make glad the City of God, the Holy Place of the Most High. God is in the midst of her. She shall not be moved. He uttered His voice, the Earth melted. The Lord of Hosts is with us; the God of Jacob is our refuge. Come, behold the works of the Lord, what desolations He hath made in the Earth. He maketh wars to cease unto the ends of the Earth; He breaketh the bow, and cutteth the spear in sunder; He burneth the chariot in the fire. Be still, and know that I AM God: I will be exalted among the heathen, I will be exalted in the Earth. The Lord of Host is with us; the God of Jacob is our refuge."

III. The Light Represents The Divine's Presence

Why was the cloud important? The cloud was important because the cloud symbolized God's presence with His people. The huge and striking cloud gave off light where there was not an abundance of light. And the cloud clearly identifies the presence of the Lord with them. The cloud assured them of the *with-us-ness* presence of God. And His presence assures them of His provisions. He is Jehovah-Jireh. He is the God who provides.

So, when Jesus says, "I AM the Light of the World," He is promising us His presence and His provision. You see, this world ain't just dark, but it's dangerous. I know that Mary J. Blige sings, "No More Drama," but I came to tell us that Mary J's song might be pretty, but the theology is off. For if you follow Jesus, there's going to be some more drama. There's going to be drama here, drama there, everywhere, drama. There's going to be dark drama, and there's going to be some dangerous drama. But in the midst of drama that's dark and dangerous, we don't have to go to pieces because the Lord is with us and His presence not only dispels darkness, but it dispels fear.

To show you that the Lord is with us, you can't spell Jesus without including "us." And because He's with us, whatever we need, just ask. So, because He's present with us, in the midst of danger and darkness, we can say like David, "I will fear no evil for Thou art with me." That's why we can sing, "Be not dismayed, whate'er betide, God will take care of you.

Let me close by telling us that Jesus the Light of the World is present and doesn't just want to be with us and protect us, but He wants to be present within us. Jesus, the Light of the World said in Matthew 5:13, "Ye are the Light of the World." He wants to be present in us. Therefore, He shares His light with us. That's why we can sing, "This little light of mine, I'm gonna let it shine." All in my heart. All in my neighborhood. Everywhere I go. Jesus gave it to me.

But while you are trying to let your light shine, Satan will try to put it out, but he can't. So, just keep on singing. In Matthew 28:20, Jesus said, "Lo, I AM with you always, even unto the end of the world."

Hebrews 13:5 is a palindrome promise. To help us understand palindrome, let me explain: Level spelled forward is level, and spelled backwards is level. That's the way Hebrews 13:5 is. You can read it forward or backwards, and it means the same. I will never leave thee nor forsake thee." The Lord, the Light, has promised to be with us.

3

"I AM the Door"

John 10:7 (KJV) - *⁷ Then said Jesus unto them again, "Verily, verily, I say unto you, I am the door of the sheep."*

One of the literary techniques of John was to have Jesus make a statement, and the person or persons to whom He speaks altogether misses His meaning. Then, Jesus has to go back and explain that which was not spiritually discerned. He did it in John 3 with Nicodemus, who failed to grasp what it means to be born again. He did it in John 4 with the woman at the well who did not understand what Jesus meant by living water. He even had to do that in John 11 with His own disciples when they failed to understand Him when He said that Lazarus was asleep.

And here, in John chapter 10, Jesus seeks to expose and unravel misunderstood mysteries. John chapter 10 is an aftermath of what takes place in chapter 9. In John chapter 9, Jesus gave the man born blind his sight. This caused the Pharisees to become irate. As a result, seeking to get rid of the evidence, thus discrediting the miracle, they confronted the man's parents. And then they asked the man himself, seeking an explanation about how one who was born blind could now see. The parents answered in fear. They said, "Ask him. He's of age." When they asked the healed man, the healed man confessed the fact that it was it out, but he can't. So, just keep on singing. In Matthew 28:20, Jesus said, "Lo, I AM with you always, even unto the end of the world."

Hebrews 13:5 is a palindrome promise. To help us understand palindrome, let me explain: Level spelled forward is level, and spelled backwards is level. That's the way Hebrews 13:5 is. You can read it forward or backwards, and it means the same. I will never leave thee nor forsake thee." The Lord, the Light, has promised to be with us.

3

"I AM the Door"

John 10:7 (KJV) - *⁷ Then said Jesus unto them again, "Verily, verily, I say unto you, I am the door of the sheep."*

One of the literary techniques of John was to have Jesus make a statement, and the person or persons to whom He speaks altogether misses His meaning. Then, Jesus has to go back and explain that which was not spiritually discerned. He did it in John 3 with Nicodemus, who failed to grasp what it means to be born again. He did it in John 4 with the woman at the well who did not understand what Jesus meant by living water. He even had to do that in John 11 with His own disciples when they failed to understand Him when He said that Lazarus was asleep.

And here, in John chapter 10, Jesus seeks to expose and unravel misunderstood mysteries. John chapter 10 is an aftermath of what takes place in chapter 9. In John chapter 9, Jesus gave the man born blind his sight. This caused the Pharisees to become irate. As a result, seeking to get rid of the evidence, thus discrediting the miracle, they confronted the man's parents. And then they asked the man himself, seeking an explanation about how one who was born blind could now see. The parents answered in fear. They said, "Ask him. He's of age." When they asked the healed man, the healed man confessed the fact that it was

Jesus who indeed had opened his eyes. Upon hearing that, they cast this man out of the synagogue.

When Jesus received the news about this man being excommunicated from the synagogue, He went and found the man and began revealing to the man that He was the Eternal Son of God. At the conclusion of the Lord's revelation, the man openly confessed Jesus by saying, "Lord, I believe." What this means is that the Pharisees threw the blind beggar out of the synagogue, but Jesus led him out of the field of Judaism and into the Messianic field.

Chapter 10 becomes the chronological continuation of the story where Jesus found the man who had been healed of blindness and had been excommunicated from the synagogue because he spoke so boldly about Christ.

Though excommunicated from the synagogue, Christ led him into His Messianic fold. So, in chapter 10, Jesus seeks to make sure that the Pharisees, those who excommunicated the healed man, those pseudo-leaders, and teachers who pose as men who see and know, become obviously aware that they do not see and do not know. As a result, Jesus gives the parable about the Good Shepherd. However, verse 6 says that they do not understand His illustration. Because of their failure to grasp Jesus' parable about the Good Shepherd, He gives a parable within a parable.

Let me just say that what is presented here is not the same type of parable that we find in the synoptic gospels. For the synoptic gospels, parables are expended similes with an expressed comparison. But in John, parables are allegorical extended metaphors with implied comparisons.

In order to understand the Parable of the Good Shepherd and this parable within a parable, there are some things and some characters that must be identified:

1. The sheepfold is Judaism.
2. The thief represents the false shepherds or the religious authorities of Israel who seek to steal sheep cunningly.

3. The robber is the false shepherd of Israel who used ecclesiastical tyranny and violence to take sheep. Together, the thieves and robbers represent Israel's shepherds who feed themselves but do not feed the sheep.
4. The porter, who signifies the one who vouched and presented the shepherd, has a twofold meaning. On the one hand, it refers to John the Baptist, but ultimately, on the other hand, it refers to the Holy Spirit.
5. The sheep are the elect of God within Judaism who hear the voice of Christ and respond positively to His call.
6. The Shepherd and the Door represent Jesus the Christ.

To further understand this parable, I think it is necessary that we understand the fact that there were two kinds of sheepfolds, which was the communal property of the native farmers which consisted of an enclosure with walls 10 to 12 feet high. When night came, a number of different shepherds would lead their sheep into the sheepfold in the care of the porter while they went and lodged for the night. The porter would care for the sheep at night, and then in the morning, each shepherd would come and call their sheep by name and lead them out to pasture.

The other kind of sheepfold was found on the countryside. It was nothing more than a circle of rocks or thorn bushes into which the sheep could be driven. To this fold, there was no door, just an opening. And what would happen was, the shepherd would place his body across that opening. The sheep could neither go out nor come in unless they crossed over his body. In a very real sense, he literally becomes the living door.

Again, let me reiterate the fact that after Jesus gave the parable on the Good Shepherd, the Jews, who supposedly both see and know, failed to understand the meaning of the Good Shepherd story. So, because of their failure to discern His symbolic language, He then plainly and without concealment, seeks to illustrate His Good Shepherd parable.

Hence, Jesus gives this parable within a parable to expose the meaning of the un-grasped parable. In the parable, Jesus moves from being a shepherd to being a door. I think I should say that there are three different doors. Not only are there two kinds of sheepfolds, but there are also three different kinds of doors in the Text.

In verse 1, the door was God's appointed way for the Shepherd to go into Judaism. In verse 7, the door was God's way for Christ to lead His elect out of Judaism. But then in verse 9, the door has to do with Salvation for Jews and Gentiles. So, the door represents both the door of exit and the door of entrance. The question is, what does it mean for Jesus to say, "I AM the Door?"

I. The Sole Means of Access

For Jesus to say, "I AM the Door," means that Jesus is the sole way whereby alienated men have access into the presence of God. Because of the original sin of Adam, every man, by nature, is separated and alienated by God. Because of sin, there is a barrier, a chasm, and a breach between God and Man. Because of sin, Man has been barred from the presence of the Holy and Righteous God. Because of sin, Man is tainted and defiled, thereby, creating a guilty distance between God and Man.

But, though there is separation and distance between God and man, and though sin has barred us from the presence of God, God was not satisfied with the gap that sin and guilt had caused. God was sorely displeased with the chasm and the gulf that existed between God and Man, the Creator and His creation. To prove His dissatisfaction, God took the initiative to bridge the gap and the spanning chasm.

God had a divine plan for reconciliation. The plan was that Jesus was sent by God to bridge the gulf, the gap, the chasm that existed between God and Man. That's why we read "God was in Christ, reconciling the world unto Himself." That's why we read, "But now in Christ Jesus ye who sometimes were afar off are made nigh by the blood of Christ." That's why we read, "For when we were without strength, in due time, Christ died for the ungodly." And then, "But God commendeth His love toward us, in that while we were yet sinners, Christ died for us." And finally, "When we were enemies, we were reconciled to God by the death of His son."

God wants us to have access to Him. God knew that of ourselves, we could not enter into His holy presence because we were dead in trespasses and sins. So, Christ was sent to be our provisionary means to Him. That was God's divine plan for reconciliation. As a result, if we seek to come to God, we must come through the door. And the door is Jesus. So, Jesus is the door of exit from sin, but He is also the door of entrance to God.

However, it is a sad commentary that Christ has said, "I AM the Door," and yet, Man is so arrogant that he seeks pseudo-alternatives. Like the Jews who tried Judaism's law, works, and circumcision, the autonomy of the individual is a dominant philosophical idea today. We all have a human quest for autonomy. As a result, we modernists are trying our pseudo-alternatives. We are trying secular humanism, moralism, positive thinking, reason, meditation, birthright, family descent, open external profession without internal possession, joining the church without joining Jesus, and being baptized in the water but not in the Blood.

I want to tell us that these are ways that seem right. And ways that seem right ultimately lead to destruction. I want to reaffirm the fact that there is only one way. There is exclusive *only-ness* here. There is no other way. Jesus is the exclusive, only way. Can't you hear Him saying, "I AM the Way, the Truth, and the Life: no man cometh unto the Father but by Me"?

In Noah's day, there was only one door to the Ark which represented salvation from destruction. Then, there was only one door to the Tabernacle, which was God's dwelling place in the wilderness. And in like fashion, there is only one door of reconciliation whereby we might enter into the presence of God, and Jesus is that door.

I would like to show us what it says by showing us what it does not say. Jesus does not say, "I Am the wall." But He says, "I AM the door." What this says is that in order for us to enter the presence of

God, there are no difficult walls for us to scale. There is nothing hard or difficult. There's nothing complex and complicated. There's nothing sophisticated involved here. We don't have to know calculus and trigonometry. We don't have to be computer literate. We don't have to unravel some complex scientific formula, some philosophical dogma, or decipher some theological jargon. We don't have to have a certain amount of logical inductive of deductive apriorist reasoning. We can be unlettered and unlearned and still have access to God. Because with Christ being the Door, all we have to do is step in. We don't even have to knock because the Door is open. Just step in.

There is a tragedy here, and the tragedy is, as Fredrick Buechner says, there are those who are "locked in a room with an open door." We are locked in the room of sin, and yet, the door to hope and to life everlasting is wide open. And I think I need to tell somebody, that if you have not stepped in, I would step in today while the Door is open. Today is the day of Salvation. Right now, Jesus is the calling Shepherd and the open Door. But one day, the day of Salvation will give way to the day of wrath. One day, the open Door of entrance will be the closed Door of exclusion. The open Door of invitation will become the closed Door of damnation. And on that day, Jesus will no longer be the calling Shepherd and the open Door, but He will be the feared, divine bartender and He will be serving the wine of wrath from the goblet of retributive justice. And on that day, just like the door of the Ark was shut, the Door of invitation will be shut. And when the Door of invitation shuts and becomes the Door of exclusion, there will be no more chances to have access to God.

When the Door of invitation shuts and becomes the Door of exclusion, there will be no more mercy, grace, salvation, regeneration, justification, sanctification, or glorification, just the unleashing of God's wrath. And God's wrathful attitude will issue forth into judgmental action. And God's judgmental action will result in eternal separation and condemnation. So, if I were you, I would step into the door today while the Shepherd is calling and the door of invitation is open.

II. He Is the Sole Entry

Because Jesus is the Door, by the enablement of Christ, any man can enter. Listen to what Jesus said, "I AM the Door: by Me, if any man enter, he shall be saved." By Jesus being the sole entryway, that says that the Door of invitation is open and available to any man. And that's good news because we live in a world that is acquainted with partiality, favoritism, prejudice, segregation, and biases. In our modern culture, in order to be in some things, and in order to get some things, you must be a certain age, or in a certain race, or a certain party, or a certain social class, or caste system, or in a certain income bracket, or a certain profession, or a certain occupation, or a certain ethnic group.

The story is, that in the days of slavery, some foreigners visited America and went to a Black school and marveled as Black children said the Pledge of Allegiance. The foreigners, knowing the harshness, cruelty, and inhumanity of slavery, marveled at how those Black children said, "With liberty and justice for all." The principal responded to the marveling of the foreigners by saying, "But what you can't hear is what they are saying underneath their breath. Underneath their breath, they say, 'With liberty and justice for all but me.'"

And I'm like those little children, there are some things that are for everybody, but me. There are some closed circles that are for everybody, but me. Amid a society that is bent on being prejudiced, covertly racist, biased, and partial where it's for everybody, but me, Jesus comes with good news. He comes with an invitation that is non-restrictive. It's an "even me" invitation. And that's good news.

To let you know the sincerity and seriousness of this all-inclusive, catholic, "even me" invitation, you will notice that this non-restrictive emphasis is everywhere. Jesus said in Matthew 11:28, "Come unto me all ye that labor and are heavy laden, and I will give you rest. Take my yoke upon you and learn of me; for I AM meek and lowly in heart: and ye shall find rest unto your souls. For my yoke is easy, and my burden is light." Jesus said, "If any man will come after Me, let him deny himself, and take up his cross, and follow Me." Jesus said, "I AM the living bread which came down from heaven: if any man eat of this bread, he shall live forever." Jesus said, "If any man thirsts, let him come unto Me, and drink." Jesus said, "If any man serve Me, let him follow Me." Jesus said, "If any man serve Me, him will My Father honor." Paul said, "Therefore, if any man be in Christ, he is a new creature: old things are passed away; behold, all things are become new." Revelation 3:20 says, "Behold, I stand at the door and knock: if any man hear My voice and open the door, I will come unto him, and will sup with him, and he with Me."

There is no partiality or prejudice involved here. It's available to all, "even me." Dr. D. Edwin Johnson used to say, "No matter what your age bracket is, the active adolescents, tender teens, teachable twenties, tireless thirties, forceful forties, fierceful fifties, seasoned sixties, septuagenarian seventies, octogenarian eighties, non-nagenerian nineties, or centenarian hundreds, all men, like Lazarus, are candidates for instant resurrection.

And the marvel is, the Lord knows that we have a God-sized void in our lives. The Lord also knows that we don't have the sense nor the inner motivation to seek to walk through the Door. So, the same Jesus who extends the invitation is the same Jesus who promises divine enablement. He says, "By Me." Jesus is not only the Door, but He is the Calling Shepherd, the Divine Enabler, and the Moving Force that enables us to respond to His call and walk through the Door. He's calling, waiting, and available with His help. And with His inviting and enabling power, we are able to walk:

From darkness to light,
From sin to Salvation,
From existence to essence,
From the old life to New life,
From ruptured relationships to reconciliation,
From the carnal to the spiritual,
From estrangement to fellowship,
From despair to hope,

From an enemy to an heir,
From wrath to righteousness,
From lost to found,
From blindness to sight,
From damnation to regeneration,
From war to peace,
From death to life,
From ruin to redemption,
From depravity to deliverance,
From defeat to victory,
From bondage to freedom,
From enslavement to liberty,
From a child of the Devil to an adopted Son of God, and
From destined to Hell to assured of Heaven.

You can't do it on your own. Jesus said, "Without me, ye can do nothing. With God, and by Me," all things are possible. Paul said, "I can do all things through Christ which strengtheneth me." That's why we can sing:

He walks with me,
And talks with me,
And tells me that I am His own.
And the joy we share,
As we tarry there,
None other has ever known.

III. The Sole Means of Benefits

Because Jesus is the door, when you enter the door, you shall be saved and shall go in and out, and find pasture. This latter part gives us the great benefits of entering God's flock through the Door, Jesus Christ.

The first benefit is that YOU SHALL BE SAVED. Now, originally, salvation meant to make safe or to deliver from a threat; it meant the dynamic act of snatching somebody from danger; it meant keeping somebody in safety; it meant to benefit somebody, or to keep them in good health. It had reference to deliverance from danger, distress, enemies, and bondage. This word basically had reference to the preservation of inner and outer safety.

Now, in the New Testament, *saved* or *salvation* refers to God's gracious work that is wrought in human lives, whereby an individual is saved from the penalty of sin, the power of sin, and ultimately, from the presence of sin. This salvation is past, present, and future. This salvation is instant, progressive, and ultimate. This salvation originates with God, it's appropriated through Christ, and incited by the Holy Spirit. And it is all of grace. In this salvation, the man who, by faith, believes in the redemptive work of God in Christ, focusing on the death, burial, and resurrection of Jesus, is delivered from sin and death, guilt and estrangement, ignorance of the truth, bondage and vice, the fear of Death and Hell, the despair of self, alienation from God, and meaningless life. This salvation means that you receive acquittal and justification before God. You are reconciled to God. Your sins have been atoned for. You have experienced inner transformative metamorphosis that is so radical until it is called, "The New Birth." You experience the power of the Holy Spirit within. You receive peace and joy. All things become new. It takes is believing childlike trust in Jesus to walk through the Door, and you shall be saved.

I want to parenthetically say that it is impossible to be on both sides of the Door because the Door is a Door of division and separation. So, you are either inside the Door, or outside of the Door. I'm glad to testify that I'm inside the Door of separation. To be inside the Door of separation means that you are saved!

The second benefit is that YOU SHALL BE SAFE. Jesus said, "And shall go in and out." This phrase is really not about entering and leaving at your own discretion and pleasure, but this phrase is a Hebrew idiom. To be able to come in and go out unmolested was a Jewish way of describing a life that was safe and secure. We find these words in Deuteronomy 28:6, for it says, "Blessed shalt thou be when thou comest in, and blessed shalt thou be when goest out." We find it again in I Kings 3:7, for Solomon said, "I am but a little child: I know not how to go out or come in." We see it again in Psalm 121:8, "The Lord shall preserve thy going out and thy coming in from this time forth, and even forevermore." To go in and out meant peace. So, the point is that Jesus promises safety for those who come through the door.

To know that the Lord will keep us safe is good news. Like sheep, we are surrounded by enemies and predators. Like sheep, we must deal with danger. The rapper Mystikal rapped about "Danger," but he's talking about dancing and sex. As a believer, our danger is from another realm. Paul, in Romans 8, lists seven forces arrayed against us: (1) trouble, (2) hardship, (3) persecution, (4) famine, (5) nakedness, (6) danger, and (7) the sword. But in the midst of danger and forces arrayed against us, we don't have to be scared because Jesus is not only the Door, but the defender of the sheep and He has all power at His disposal, and He is able to protect us from all hurt and harm, dangers seen and unseen.

The story is that there was an airplane that was flying 37,000 feet in the midst of a horrible storm. Everybody on board was fearful and panic-stricken with the exception of one little boy in first class. The man who was seated by the boy noticed the unusual calmness about this boy. So, the man asked the boy, "Aren't you scared like the rest of us?" The boy said, "No." The man asked, "Why aren't you scared like the rest of us? We are in a storm and we could perish in this storm. Why is it that you are so calm?" The boy said, "The reason that I'm calm and not scared is because my father is the pilot, and I have the faith in my father that he's going to land this plane safely."

Like this boy, I've been in the storm and rain, but I'm not scared because Jesus, The Door, is the pilot. He's leading me. David said, "The Lord is my Shepherd." He's in front, but He's following me. "Surely goodness and mercy shall follow me all the days of my life." But He's beside me. The Holy Spirit is the Paraclete – He's the one called alongside. All night, and all day, angels keep watch over me. So, I don't have to be afraid. All I've got to do is lean on Him.

I'm not scared. I'm safe and secure. I'm not scared. God is our refuge and strength, a very present help in trouble. I'm not scared. I will lift up mine eyes unto the hills from whence cometh my help. I'm not scared. The Lord is my light and my salvation. I'm not scared. I'm safe and secure. I've seen the lightning flashing, and I heard the thunder roll. I've felt sin breakers dashing trying to conquer my soul. I heard the voice of Jesus telling me still to fight on. He promised never to leave me. Never to leave me alone. I'm not scared. I'm safe and secure.

That's why I love the song that says, "What a fellowship, what a joy divine, leaning on the everlasting arms. What a blessedness, what a peace is mine, leaning on the everlasting arms. What have I to dread? What have I to fear? Leaning on the everlasting arms. I have blessed peace, with my Lord so near, leaning on the everlasting arms. Leaning, leaning, safe and secure from all alarm. Leaning, leaning, leaning on the everlasting arms."

I'm not scared. That's why I can sing, "Be not dismayed, what 'ere betide; God will take care of you. Beneath His wings of love abide; God will take care of you."

4

"I AM the Good Shepherd"

John 10:11 (KJV) - *¹¹ I am the good shepherd: the good shepherd giveth his life for the sheep.*

A careful examination of the life of Jesus readily reveals that Jesus never made the blunder of speaking a language that His hearers were unable to grasp. He was never accused of over-shooting His audience. Jesus was never guilty of speaking too far above the level of the comprehension of His audience. He was never caught up in the vacuum where He wanted to be so immaculately polished that when He finished, people neither understood what He was saying nor had they the foggiest notion as to what the Gospel was all about. Jesus was unlike some of our modern proclaimers. You see, some modern proclaimers want to be intellectually impressive. They want to leave men baffled with their brilliance, but being intellectually impressive was not the aim of Jesus. The aim of Jesus was to prick men's conscience and convict their hearts.

Also, Jesus had to have been a master rhetorician. This had to have been true, for it is evidenced by the fact that His speaking at the age of 12 stymied and dumbfounded doctors and lawyers. And then too, being the God-man, Jesus was both Omniscient and Omnisapient, meaning

He's All-Knowing and All-Wise. But, Jesus seemed to be used of God by the impression that the Gospel was to clarify men rather than mystify men. Consequently, Jesus spoke a language that could readily and easily be interpreted by His listeners. Like Himself, He spoke with such clarity and charming simplicity that His words became flesh, available for all to behold. Jesus also spoke a language the people could identify.

Housewives could identify with leaven. Vinedressers could identify with vines, branches, and fruit. Farmers could identify with harvests, wheat, tares, sowing, and reaping. Ranchers could identify with shepherds, sheep, goats, and wolves. Fishermen could identify with fishing and nets. Parents could identify with children. Men could identify with fathering. Women could identify with virgins. The poor could identify with the laborers and beggars. Children could identify with dogs and crumbs. Kings could identify with kingdoms and servants. Masters could identify with slaves. The rich could identify with purple and fine linen. And all men could identify with salt, light, and cities.

Our Text is a classic example of Jesus speaking a language His hearers could identify with. When Jesus used the picture of the shepherd and the sheep, Jesus was using a picture that was woven into the thoughts and the language of the Jewish people. The main part of Judea is the central plateau. It is rough with little grass making it naturally a pastoral country. Therefore, the most familiar figure of the Judean uplands was that of the shepherd. So, what Jesus did was to take the picture of the shepherd, a picture that was deeply woven into the imagery and language of the people, and made it the picture of Himself.

This statement grows out of a miracle that Jesus performed. The Lord opened the eyes of the blind man. The people, in turn, brought the man to the Pharisees, who were the religious authorities. As the man talked to them, he began to grow in wisdom. Because of the fact that He spoke so well, so bravely, and so boldly in defense of Jesus based upon what He knew. John reports that the Pharisees became vexed and angry to the point that they excommunicated the healed man from the synagogue. This means that they excommunicated him from worship and fellowship. When Jesus found out that the man had been excommunicated, He went and found him. Recognizing the man had been cast out and abused, Jesus goes to him for the purpose of encouraging and comforting him.

Jesus seeks to assure the healed man that he was unjustly rejected and cast out by men, but there is a friend that none could debar him from. He wants, seemingly, to impress upon the mind of this man the fact that, though persecutors may exclude healed men from their communion, they cannot exclude them from the communion of Christ. So, when Jesus found the man, Jesus exposed who He was to the man, and then asked, in effect, "Do you believe in me?" The man responded by saying, "I believe in you." In the midst of this short conversation, Jesus says of Himself, "I AM the Good Shepherd."

Note, Jesus does not say I AM a good shepherd, but He says that "I AM the Good Shepherd." For Jesus to say, "I AM" means Jesus has taken a backward leap and has linked Himself to that mystic incommunicable name Jehovah, which was so sacred until it was only pronounced once a year, and that was by the high priest on the day of atonement in the most holy place. "I AM" directly links Jesus to God. Remember the God-Moses encounter on the back side of the desert, when at the Burning Bush, on holy ground, God said to Moses, "Go to Egypt and tell Pharaoh to let my people go." And Moses said, "Lord, whom shall I say sent me?" God responded by saying, "Tell them that I AM hath sent thee." Tell them, I AM that I AM." So, when Jesus says, "I AM," what He is really saying is I AM Yahweh-Jesus. And what He is saying is, as Yahweh, I made the world, and as Jesus, I have come to save the world I made.

Jesus wants us to understand that He is inextricably tied to God, so much so, until John writes, "In the beginning was the word; and the word was with God; and the Word was God. The same was in the beginning with God. All things were made by Him, and without Him was not anything made that was made." Jesus is so tied into God that He said, "I and my Father are one. He that hath seen me hath seen the Father also. If ye had known me, ye should have known my Father also. No man cometh unto the Father, but by Me." He was so tied that Paul says, "Christ is the visible image of the invisible God. In Him dwelt all of the fullness of the Godhead bodily." Hence, Jesus used the mystical incommunicable name "I AM."

Therefore, He says, "I AM the Good Shepherd."

This simple but sublime declaration implies a profound yet practical working relationship between a human being and his Maker. This declaration links a lump of clay to Divine Destiny. This declaration suggests that a mere mortal becomes the cherished object of divine diligence. This declaration says that God in Christ is deeply concerned about every human being. This says that God is concerned about Man. Deity is concerned about dust. Glory is concerned about mud. The Regal is concerned about the rascals. The Sinless One is concerned about the sinful ones. The Heavenly is concerned about the earthly. The Eternal is concerned about the ephemeral. The Celestial is concerned about the terrestrial. In examining the text, there are at least three things that Jesus seeks to get across that are abundantly true of His shepherding.

I. The Shepherd Knows His Sheep

Verse 14 says, "I am the Good Shepherd, and I know my sheep." In the East, the relationship between the shepherd and the sheep is different from that in the West. In the West, sheep are mainly kept for killing. However, in the East, the sheep are largely kept for their milk and for their fleece for making wool. It thus happened that in the Palestine area, the sheep were often with the shepherd for some eight or nine years. The shepherd literally had a name for every sheep, and the sheep came to know their names. But being so close to the sheep for so long, the shepherd got to know the temperaments and the behaviors of the sheep. He knew which sheep were arrogant, bunning, and domineering. He knew which ones would butt and drive other lambs away from grazing. He could tell which ones were restless and discontented. He could see which ones would become irritable and lose weight. He knew which sheep were less aggressive. He knew which ones were strong or weak, stubborn or submissive. He knew them so well that he knew their hurts and their needs. A good shepherd knows his sheep.

Likewise, Jesus the Good Shepherd knows His sheep. The Lord is not an impersonal shepherd. And this is good news and bad news. It's good news because we live in an impersonal, depersonalized, numerical society. Therefore, my name does not count. My name has been lost in the maze of computer technology. Men don't want to know my name anymore. They just want to know my numbers. My license number, my social security number, my policy number, my plate number, my check number, my credit card number, my ID number, my Versatel number, my fax number, my email number, and my cell phone number. But it's comforting to know that on a day when my name does not count, my Shepherd knows me by my name. That's good news and bad news for us, for the Good Shepherd knowing us by our names is suggestive of the fact that He knows more than just our names. In those days, names and natures had to correlate. That's why some people had name changes.

So, the Lord knows not only our names but our nature. Our Shepherd is All-Knowing. He has an All-Seeing Eye, and He is the Divine Catherer. His knowledge of us is much greater than just mere intellectual awareness. And that's good news and bad news because He knows us better than we know ourselves. He knows our strengths and weaknesses. He knows our successes and failures. He knows our thoughts from afar off. I tell you that He doesn't just know our names, He knows our nature. He knows the strong, the stubborn, the submissive. i our sins and our inequities. And our iniquities are like cholesterol, the sins that come through our DNA. Our Shepherd knows:

> Who's proud – self-righteous – hypocritical,
> Who's envious – jealous,
> Who's slothful,
> Who's gluttonous,
> Who's lustful – immoral – carnal – worldly,
> Who has the lying tongue,

Who's heart devises wicked imagination,
Who's feet run swift to mischief,
Who sows discord among the brethren,
Who's wise,
Who's faithful – righteous-spiritual – godly,
Who's courageous,
Who's loving, and
Who's real.

He knows our hurts, our cares, and our needs. Solomon says, "The ways of man are before the eyes of the Lord." The Shepherd knows His sheep. He knows us because we are His, twice.

There's a story of a little boy who made himself a boat. When he tried it out, it got lost. One day, he happened to see the boat at a pawn shop. He ran and grabbed the boat. The shopowner said, "The boat is for sale." The boy tried to explain. The shop owner insisted. The little boy ran home after being told it cost $2.50. He sold some bottles and cut somebody's lawn. When he got the $2.50, he ran back, put the money on the counter, got the boat, clenched it to his chest, and said, "You are mine, boat. You are really mine. You are mine, twice. You're mine because I made you, and you are mine because I bought you."

He knows us so well that He knows our downsittings and uprisings. He knows the strands of hair on our heads. He knows what we are. He knows what we were. He knows that we are more than what we have become. He knows how much we can bear. He knows us externally and internally. I had an old deacon who used to say that God knows our needs, and He knows our "don't needs." That's good news and bad news.

There's a good reason why He knows us so well. The Good Shepherd created His sheep. Psalm 100 says, "It is He that hath made us and not we ourselves." John says, "All things were made by Him, and without Him was not anything made that was made." It was the Good Shepherd who created us, molded us, and shaped us from the dust of the ground. He knows us because He made us as God's creation. Every aspect of our being is the result of His creative genius. But as His revealed sheep, we represent the handiwork of the Shepherd. The Psalmist says that we are fearfully and wonderfully made. And to show you that we are fearfully and wonderfully made, each of us is a *first*. We are an *only edition*. There is no second edition of me. I am fearfully and wonderfully made. What all this says is that nothing in His flock is hidden from Him. Our weaknesses, our frailties, our failures, our sins, and our good (the good things about us). All are open to Him. And the sin in us did not discourage Him or weaken His love for us. In spite of us, He loves us. The Shepherd knows us.

II. The Shepherd Is With His Sheep

Verse 12 says that the hireling shepherd leaves and flees in times of danger. But conversely, when you examine verses 2 and 4, you will see that the Good Shepherd calls His sheep by name. He leads them. He goes before them. Sheep follow Him. And they know His voice. And if false shepherds flee and leave, Good Shepherds stay. That says, the Good Shepherd is with His sheep. Sheep do not take care of themselves. They require, more than any other class of livestock, endless attention, meticulous care, careful handling, and detailed direction. They need the reassuring presence of the shepherd. It is the presence of the shepherd that gives the sheep release from their fears and anxieties. Sheep will not lie down, rest, relax, be content, or be quiet if the shepherd is not around.

It is said that sheep do not have good eyesight. They can only see about 15 yards. So, in order to keep the sheep from being troubled, uneasy, and panic-stricken, the shepherd has to be near. Sheep are prone to wander. So, in order to keep the sheep together rather than wandering and breaking away from the main flock, the shepherd has to be near the sheep. It is said that in the East, in when the shepherd desires to recline and rest, knowing that he can only sleep with one eye closed and both ears open, he fixes his staff upright in the ground and arranges his coat on it. He also has his headgear on top, so that when the sheep glance upward it gives the illusion that the shepherd is still with them. Likewise, the golden thread of comfort and sustenance that runs throughout the Bible from the beginning to the end is the fact that God is with us.

Jacob, when he was dying, told Joseph, "Behold I die: but God shall be with you." The Lord's message to Moses was, "My presence shall go with thee." God told Joshua, "As I was Moses, so will I be with thee." Elisha told the fearful servant, "They that be with us are more than they that be with them." David said, "Yea, though I walk through the valley of the shadow of death, I will fear no evil for Thou art with me." Isaiah 41:10 says, "Fear thou not; for I am with thee: be not dismayed; for I AM thy God: I will strengthen thee; yea, I will help thee; yea, I will uphold thee with the right hand of my righteousness." Isaiah 43:2 says, "When thou passest through the water, I will be with thee." The Lord said to Jeremiah, "Be not afraid of their faces: for I am with thee to deliver thee." The title "Emmanuel" means, "God with us." Paul leaves this witness with Timothy. "Demas, having loved this present world, hath forsaken me, and departed to Thessalonica; Alexander the coppersmith has done me much harm; notwithstanding, the Lord stood with me."

Just before Jesus boarded the Mt. Olive cloud, He said to His disciples, "Go ye therefore, and teach all nations, baptizing them in the name of the Father and of the Son and of the Holy Ghost: teaching them to observe all things whatsoever I have commanded you: and lo, I AM with you always, even unto the end of the earth."

Jesus had this to say to His bewildered and grief-stricken disciples, "And I will pray the Father, and He shall give you another comforter, that He may abide with you forever." It is a fact that the Lord is with us. To show us His *with-us-ness presence*, He is in front of us as our Shepherd, leading us. He is in the back of us with goodness and mercy. He is on the side of us. He is our Paraclete. He is:

With us in every situation.
With us in every dark trial.
With us in the midst of dismal disappointments.

With us in every distressing dilemma.
With us in every crisis.
With us in every chilling circumstance.
With us in the midst of emotional exposure.
With us in adversities.
With us when predators attack.
With us when dark shadows sweep.
With us when we slump in deep despair.
With us when the path we trod seems gloomy.
With us when rivers reverse.
With us when the water overflows the banks.
With us when storms break out.

In Hebrews 13:5, He gives us a palindrome promise, "I will never leave thee nor forsake thee." Since I gave to Jesus my poor broken heart, He never has left me alone.

III. The Shepherd Dies for His sheep

Sheep have enemies that annoy, distract, and torment them. They are nasal flies, warble flies, and ticks. But then sheep have enemies who do more than distract and annoy. There are wolves, dogs, coyotes, cougars, bears, lions, snakes, and lizards. Sheep are clean, harmless, gentle, helpless, and dependent creatures. Sheep have little or no means of self-defense. Sheep are timid and feeble creatures whose only recourse is to run, stand still, or be devoured. The Shepherd represents the main source of defense for the sheep. Likewise, we have enemies., the Devil, the world, and the flesh. For we wrestle not against flesh and blood, but against principalities, against powers, against the rulers of the darkness of this world, against spiritual wickedness in high places. And our Shepherd represents our main protection.

But let me show us how the Good Shepherd differs from all the other shepherds. Ordinary shepherds risk their lives in defense of their sheep. But they do not actually lay their lives down. They do not yield their lives as a voluntary sacrifice. And if they did, it would be fatal for the shepherdless sheep.

But where Jesus is concerned, for Him to lay down His life is not fatal and disastrous to the fold. But it is beneficial to the fold. Under the old dispensation, the sheep dies for the shepherd. But under the new dispensation, the Good Shepherd dies for the sheep.

In verses 11, 15, 17-18, five times He affirms the sacrificial nature of His death. Which means that Jesus did not die a martyr, killed by men. The Jews did not kill Jesus. The Romans did not kill Jesus. Jesus said, "No man takes My life. I have power to lay it down, and I have power to take it up again." From a human standpoint, Jesus was executed. But from the divine side, let me tell us the real truth. Jesus died as a substitute, willingly laying down His life for His sheep. Jesus said in John 15:13, "Greater love hath no man than this, that a man lay down his life for his friends." And Jesus is the only Shepherd who saves the sheep by laying down His life. You see, when Jesus vicariously died in our stead, the sheep benefited from that substitutionary death.

Now, let me tell us how and why He died. The fact is that the enemy got in the sheepfold, and when he got through with us, we were in bad shape. The enemy didn't annihilate us, but he did ruin us. For when the enemy got through, he left us cut asunder, fractured, fragmented, separated, estranged, divested, stripped, splintered, split apart, denuded. In other words, we did not look like God anymore, but before Man could complete his spiritual destruction or before Man conformed and was left to the damnation that he had chosen, I hear the Good Shepherd saying to His Shepherd Father—Father if you will prepare Me a body that will shed forth blood and water, I will catch the boat of destruction. I'll come down through 42 burning generations. I'll ride the nine-month train and get off at a little town called Bethlehem of Judea. I'll stay in the world for 33 years. But one day, I'll lay down My life for My sheep. I'll go to Calvary and die.

But I want to close by telling you that on Friday, Jesus died as the Good Shepherd, but early Sunday morning He rose as the Great Shepherd!

5

"I AM the Resurrection and the Life"

John 11:25 (KJV) - *²⁵ Jesus said to her, "I am the resurrection and the life. The one who believes in me will live, even though they die."*

One of the most precious things in life is to have somewhere to go where the tensions of life are relaxed and where you can be at peace. It is refreshing to have a circle and a fellowship where you can go and open your mind and heart and be assured that you will never be laughed at or misunderstood. Jesus had such a place in the home of Mary, Martha, and Lazarus. I can imagine that in Jesus' case, such a place must have been doubly sweet and valuable, for He admitted that He had nowhere to lay His head and no place to call home.

From that home, Jesus received some bad news. It is interesting to note that though Jesus had no permanent address, Mary and Martha knew how to get a hold of Him.

When Jesus received the news, He was on a two or three-day journey from Bethany which is two miles from Jerusalem. He was such a distance away because things had become dangerous for Him, and the situation had become so serious that He was compelled to retire from

Jerusalem and take refuge on the other side of the Jordan. The Jewish authorities were so enraged against Him that they attempted to stone Him to death.

Knowing that His "Hour had now come," Jesus withdrew from the area of Jerusalem. While He was on the other side of the Jordan, news came to Him that His friend was seriously and gravely ill. Undoubtedly, Lazarus had been ill for some time and evidently had grown progressively worse. Apparently, the sisters had done all that they could do for him, but all of their feeble efforts were to no avail. Consequently, they sent a messenger to Jesus, telling Him about Lazarus' condition.

The message that these two sisters sent to Jesus was remarkable. It merely states, "Lord, behold, he whom Thou lovest is sick." The message does not say how sick Lazarus is. There is no direct appeal for help. It is left totally up to Jesus as to what to do. Incidentally, they did not rest their case on Lazarus' love for Jesus. They rested their case entirely on Jesus' love for Lazarus. It seems that love, affection, and attachment would dictate the moves of Jesus.

However, the moves of Jesus are troubling. He loves Lazarus. Because of His Omniscience, He knows how sick Lazarus is, and he is getting helplessly worse and will eventually die. Yet, He remains for two more days after receiving this news.

We would assume with confidence that hearing of their sore trouble, Jesus would put everything aside and hurry to their help. Most would expect Jesus to say, "My friends need Me, and I must go." And yet, this was not the case. The response of Jesus seems to be wholly out of character. What a strange reaction for divine love. It is strange because all through the Gospels one is struck by Jesus' eagerness to help. However tired He was, no claimant was ever turned away.

Oftentimes we see that before the petitioner could state his case and make his plea, Jesus was already on His feet saying, "Let us go at once." But the puzzling and bewildering question is, why did Jesus delay? There is something strange about the seeming tardiness of Jesus. Why did Jesus delay and dally? Why does He not come at once?

What we must come to grips with is the fact that Our Lord is sovereign. He moves according to His own sovereign providential plan and purpose. And because of who He is, He does not have to explain His movement. And because "His ways are not our ways, and His thoughts are not our thoughts." If He did explain them, because our reason is perverted, we possibly would not understand. Then, there are are times when God makes us trust Him in the dark.

The other night, Susaun, Sydne, Janina, and Kylie went with me to hear Dr. Rudolph McKissick. It was dark when we left the church in Compton, and we went towards the 710 freeway. It was closed, however, there were detour signs. After making several turns following the detour signs, Susaun said, "Daddy, I don't have a clue where I am." Keep in mind, that it's dark, and it's almost 11:00 pm. We were on our way to downtown L.A. and Susaun thought I had made a wrong turn because the area resembled San Pedro. She said, "This looks like San Pedro." Janina, however, said, "Well I ain't worried because I know he knows where he's going."

There are times when we must be like that with God. We must say, "God, I don't have a clue where I am. I don't know where You are leading me, but I know that You know where You are, and where You are going." We've got to get to a point with God where we say, "God, even though I can't trace your hand, I will trust Your heart." Knowing that God has a heart of love, I can interpret His delays in the light of His love. I can label these delays, of love.

Another fact that we must deal with is God's delays are not necessarily God's denials. There are times when God delays because He knows that we are not ready to receive some blessings. There are some blessings that God has to ready us for. There are some blessings, if we get them too soon, we will soon forget God. Look at the fact that it took Israel 40 years to get ready for the Promised Land. There are some blessings that God wills for us, but we are not yet mature enough to handle. There are some things that we are just too immature for.

So, don't get an attitude with God in the interim. Let God mature you so that when the blessing comes, you won't let the blessing handle you, and make you forget God. Handle the blessing and give God the Glory.

I know that this is the now, at once, generation. But God says, "There are some things that we must wait for. So, our delays are tailored to teach us how to wait, and be patient. There are some things that you have to learn how to wait on. The Bible repeatedly enjoins us to wait.

Job 4:14 reads "All the days of my appointed time will I wait, till my change comes." Psalm 27:14 says, "Wait on the Lord: be of good courage, and He shall strengthen thine heart: wait, I say on the Lord." In Psalm 40:1, David says, "I waitedly patiently on the Lord; and He inclined unto me, and heard my cry." Psalm 62: 5 says, "My soul, wait thou only upon God." Psalm 130:5-6, "I wait for the Lord, my soul doth wait, and in His word do I hope. My soul waiteth for the Lord more than they that watch for the morning." Jeremiah writes in Lamentation 3:25, "The Lord is good unto them that wait for Him." And verse 26 says, "It is good that a man should both hope and quietly wait for the salvation of the Lord." Michah 7:7 reads, "I will wait for the God of my salvation." Then, James 1:3 says that "the trying of your faith worketh patience." Isaiah 40:31 says, "But they that wait upon the Lord shall renew their strength; they shall mount up on wings as eagles; they shall run, and not be weary; they shall walk and not faint." So, we must learn how to wait. Old people used to say, "You can't hurry God; you have to learn how to wait."

What really grabs our attention is the first thing Jesus said to His disciples. Jesus said that Lazarus' sickness was not unto death. When Jesus told his disciples about the bad news that had come to Him, at first, they misunderstood Him. In noticing the writing of John, it seems to be a regular habit of John to report a conversation of Jesus with someone else, where Jesus begins with a quiet simple saying. Then, the saying is misunderstood, and then, there follows an explanation. This is the pattern in the conversation with Nicodemus. The same is true in the case of the woman at the well about the living water. Here, John writes that Jesus tells His disciples that the illness of Lazarus was not fatal. He then goes on to say that Lazarus was asleep, and that He was going to awaken him from his sleep.

To prove that the disciples misunderstood Jesus, notice that at that point, the disciples became puzzled. They well knew that sleep was the best of cures, and that sleep was the surest of all ways to recovery. To them, sleep was a sign of an abating fever. Therefore, they could not understand why Jesus would wish to awaken Lazarus. So, to clear up their misunderstanding, Jesus tells His disciples clearly and plainly, "Lazarus is dead." But the shocking statement is that Jesus, the man of compassion says, "Lazarus is dead and I'm glad." But Jesus does not bring His dialogue to a halt until he makes another statement. Jesus said, "Lazarus' situation was designed to give glory to God, that the Son of God may be glorified, and that they might believe."

What did Jesus mean by the statement that God would get glory, and that He would be glorified? First of all, the raising of Lazarus from the dead would be something that would bring glory to God by the very wonder of that happening. Then, for Jesus, this incident was going to lead to the Cross. He knew that this incident would cause the Jewish authorities to finally decide to take final action to eliminate Him. He knew that to perform such an act within two miles of the Temple and in the presence of Jerusalemites would seal His doom. Jesus knew that the need He would have to fulfill would cut across a Sadducee conviction inasmuch as they refused to believe in any life after death. He knew that when the report got out about the raising of Lazarus from the dead, a crisis would be created among the Sadducees.

So, the worldly-minded priestly aristocracy, who sought to overtake their archrival Pharisees, would seek to put an end to Jesus. And by dying on the Cross, Jesus would give glory to God.

But when Jesus has concluded, His disciples sought to lay a restraining hand upon Him. They knew that for Jesus to return to Judea was courting with certain death. They know that the authorities were set upon destroying Jesus. They know that only a few days prior, Jesus had narrowly escaped a violent and horrid death. So, they sought to dissuade Jesus from what appeared to be an insane foolhardiness that they felt might be fatal.

The anxious disciples sought to reason with Jesus, giving expressions to their fears that they felt were justified. They argued that to go back to where hostile eyes were searching for Him and where hostile hearts were plotting His doom was nothing less and nothing other than deliberate suicide. They considered it a foolish throwing away of His life. To them, it seemed suicidal madness to leave this safe retreat. They figured that even though where He was, was in the territory of Herod Antipas, it was still less perilous than Judea.

But when Jesus announced to His disciples that He was indeed going back to Judea, in spite of the hostility, the disciples were shocked and staggered. After announcing His decision to go to Judea, Thomas, the gallant pessimist, doubting but devoted, faithless but loyal, displayed a high kind of courage and encroached in loyal despair, sensing that Jesus insisted on returning, willing to go with Jesus into danger, and risk his own life, said, "Let us also go, that we may die with him."

So, Jesus set out for Bethany. When the news reaches the sorrowing household that Jesus was near, Martha ran out to meet Him. Her first words to Jesus were words of reproach and faith. Martha said, "If you had been here, my brother would not have died."

First, Jesus did not argue. He simply gave her a Divine axiom. He said, "I AM the resurrection and the life." He said, "Wherever I AM, there is life." At this point, Jesus had to lead Martha from abstract belief to personalized trust. Thus, Jesus said to Martha, "Martha, do you believe this?" Not general belief, but the specific Truths of Jesus?

Martha was specific in her response, for she uses three titles to refer to Jesus, for she said, "Yea, Lord: I believe that thou art Christ, the Son of the living God which should come into the world." Martha was specific, but I've come to realize that too many people are vague about what they believe.

A man was being questioned about what he believed as he sought to join the church. The man responded by saying, "I believe what the church believes." He said, "The church believes what I believe." The examiner asked a third question. He asked, "What do you and the church believe?" He said, "We believe the same thing."

We have too many with vague beliefs, but I thank God that I am specific. I believe in one Great God who made Heaven and Earth. I believe I was born a sinner. I believe that in love, grace, mercy, and wisdom that God sent His Son to save me. I believe His Son Jesus died a substitutionary death. And early Sunday morning, He rose for my justification. I believe in the Holy Ghost. I believe in the Bible. I believe in the Church. I believe that Jesus is coming back again.

Notice that Jesus used sorrow to teach her more of Himself And sorrow is one of the best times to learn more about Jesus. It was out of sorrow that Abraham said Jehovah Jireh, the Lord will provide. It was out of sorrow that Job said, "The Lord giveth, and the Lord taketh away." It was out of sorrow that Job said, "I know that my Redeemer liveth." It was out of sorrow that Job said again, "My witness is in Heaven,"

In sorrow, David said, "The Lord is my Shepherd. The Lord is my Light, and my salvation." It was in sorrow that Jesus said, "Let not your heart be troubled." In sorrow, you can learn about Amazing Grace. The Hymn was born in sorrow. When peace like a river attendeth my way. So, after spending a few moments comforting Martha and Mary, Jesus asked, "Where have you laid Him?" Martha proceeded to show Jesus where Lazarus was.

The tomb of Lazarus was identical to the tombs that were all over the region of Palestine. It was either a natural or artificial cave hollowed out in the rock. It was six feet long, nine feet wide, and ten feet high. It contained eight shelves, three on each side, and two on the wall facing the entrance. The tomb had no door, but in front of the opening, there ran a groove, and in the groove, there was a great stone like a card wheel and the stone was rolled across the opening to form a door which no single person could move.

When Jesus got to the tomb, the Bible say, "Jesus wept." Why? Jesus exhibits His humanity as He sorrows over the death of His friend

Lazarus. Jesus entered into all of our experiences so that when we go to Him in prayer, His first response is, "I know exactly how you feel." It is also said that Jesus wept because Jesus is God. And because Jesus is God, Jesus could see what those around Him could not see. Jesus could see Lazarus in Paradise. He could see Lazarus surrounded by the Saints of God, in the presence of Holy Angels. Lazarus had barely been introduced, and now, he must call him back. In Paradise, Lazarus was at peace in the bosom of Abraham, and now, Jesus had to recall Lazarus to a wicked world of toil, pain, sorrow, confusion, peril, trials, tribulations, conflict, and sickness, back to this world where Lazarus would have to die all over again.

The Bible says, "Jesus wept." After He weeps, He gives a command to move the stone. To Martha, this command seemed to be a useless and needless harrowing experience. She must have thought that Jesus wanted to take one last look. She could not see how there would be any consolation in viewing the grim and repulsive sight of an already putrefying corpse. For the Palestine climate, decay sat in quickly. Martha pointed out that Lazarus had already been in the tomb for four days.

The point of that was that there was the belief that the spirits of departed people were supposed to hover over the tomb for four days after death. After that, they were supposed to depart because by that time, the face of the dead person was so decayed that recognition was impossible. It was Martha's belief that Lazarus was dead beyond recall. Jesus then reinforces His command to move the stone by saying in essence, "Didn't I tell you that if you would believe, that you would see the glory of God." That question overruled Martha's objection.

Jesus does something that only Jesus can do. Jesus was praying but in His prayer, He was preaching. Jesus deliberately, openly, without pretense, and for a very good reason, preaches in His prayer. He preaches in His prayer that this public demonstration of omnipotent power would declare His oneness with the Father. And that this demonstration of power would be witnessed by those who were witnesses. It was at that moment that Jesus spoke His word of command; a command which even death was powerless to oppose. With a great voice, Jesus said, "Lazarus, come forth." It was that same Word of Power that He spoke and said, "Let there be light." It was the same Word of Power that He spoke to the sea and winds, and they obeyed. It was the same Word of Power that He spoke to demons, and they were expelled; the same Word of Power that He spoke, and lepers were cleansed; the same Word of Power that He spoke, and I got peace and joy within.

So, with a work of power, Jesus said, "Lazarus, come forth." Augustine said that it was necessary and mandatory for Jesus to call Lazarus by name. With His Word of Power, He had just said, "Come forth", and all saints would have got up out of the grave. Jesus said to the people, "You lose him and let him go." Such is the story of the raising of Lazarus.

But now, let's back up, and examine what Jesus meant when He said, "I AM the Resurrection and the Life: he that believeth in Me, though he were dead, yet shall he live again." What did Jesus mean? Is Jesus suggesting that the man who believes in Him shall come to life again? Or, is He saying that in terms of physical life, the man who believes in Him will never die? Is He saying that the man who believes in Him is immune from physical death? Is He saying that age is arrested and death stayed for the ones who believe in Him? No.

I. A Word of Salvation

Verse 26 reads, "Whosoever liveth and believeth in Me." That's salvation. Jesus is saying that a man who believes in Him is saved from death of the soul which sin brings. The point is that through Him and in Him, dead souls can and rise up out of the sleep of death, become alive, and grow sensitive, active, purposeful, and endowed with powers they did not have before.

The terms *life* and *eternal life* are the great characteristics terms of the fourth Gospel. In it, the word *life* occurs thirty-three times. Of the thirty-three, fifteen refer to eternal life. The basic purpose of the fourth Gospel is to bring men into eternal life. The Gospel of John was written to have men believe that Jesus is the Christ, the Eternal Son of God.

And by believing that Jesus is the Eternal Son of God, you may have eternal life. In saying "I AM the Resurrection and the Life," Jesus was saying that He is able to rescue men from the deadly power of sin which holds men in its grip. Physical death is no longer a terror to a man who believes in Jesus because spiritual death has been conquered.

The Bible says, "All have sinned and come short of the glory of God." Because of Adam, Man lost his innocence. We became as dead men. We were filthy. We were benumbered by vice. We were hardened like stones.

We were scarcely human. We were engulfed in a pitiless savagery. Our lives became vague, shadowy, strengthless, and joyless. We resembled specters of ghosts. We had lost all that made life worth calling it *life*. We became so insensitive that we became dead to the needs of others. We became so involved in the petty dishonesties, and petty disloyalties of life, that we became dead to honor. We became so hopeless until we became filled with inertia, which is spiritual death. We became bad men, ignorant of the fact that we could ever be better. We became totally depraved. All of our nature became tainted with sin. Our being was corrupted. Our spirits were darkened. Our souls were debased. Our bodies became diseased, and death-ridden. A schism was brought into our nature. Our hearts became deceitful. Our speech became crooked. Our attitude became perverse. We became defile and unclean. Our being was covered with spots and blemishes. We became corrupt and loathsome. The image of God was ruined. We were spiritually dead. Paul says we have become "unprofitable." And to say that we are "unprofitable" means something has gone sour and you throw that away.

But Jesus says, "I AM the Resurrection and the Life."

Jesus says, "I have the Word of Power to resurrect the life that is dead in sin." Paul raises this question, "Who shall deliver me from this deadly body?" And Paul answers the question, for he says, "Jesus Christ." And Paul is right. For Jesus Christ came into the world with the Word of Power to resurrect men from the death of sin. Jesus said, "I come that they might have life and have it more abundantly." And the man who believes in Christ receives the Word of Power to live and not fall again into this death of sin.

Jesus said in John 10:28-29, "And I give unto them eternal life; and they shall never perish; neither shall any man pluck them out of my hand. My Father which gave them me, is greater than all; and no man is able to pluck them out of my Father's hand."

The undeniable evidence that He is able to raise us up from the death of sin never to return into the death of sin is that He got up early Sunday morning with all power in His hands. When a man believes that Jesus is, and allows Jesus to resurrect Him from the death of sin, a dramatic and radical change takes place in the life of that individual that is once and for all. I'm sure that's why the songwriter wrote, "What a wonderful change in my life has been wrought since Jesus came into my heart. I have light in my soul for which love I had sought since Jesus came into my heart. I have ceased from my wandering and goings astray since Jesus came into my heart. And my sins which were many are all washed away since Jesus came into my heart."

II. A Word of Glorification

Verses 25 and 26 reads, "I AM the Resurrection and the Life: he that believeth in Me, though he were dead, yet shall he live. And whosoever liveth and believeth in Me shall not die." That's glorification. For Jesus to say that He is the Resurrection and the Life, and then to say, "shall never die," is to say that there is a certainty of life beyond death.

The Sadducees believed that there was one life after death. For many, death was the complete and inevitable end. They were convinced that nothing followed death. They believed that after death, there was nothing more than endless sleep. They were caught up in the belief that the soul perishes with the body. Many were engulfed by the attitude of Epicurus. Epicurus believed that the supreme evil in life was fear, and the greatest fear was the fear of death. He said that everything in this world was formed by a fortuitous conglomeration or concourse of primeval atoms. His theory was that in the beginning, there was nothing but atoms falling through the void of space like rain. These atoms had the power to swerve. When they swerved, they banged on and knocked into each other and became little groups. And out of the banging, chance, haphazard groups, or conglomerations of atoms, everything was formed, even the soul of Man. So, his theory was that when a man died, all that happened was that the atoms diffused and that Man ceased to be.

What he suggested was atoms thou art, to atoms thou shall return. The doctrine of the Sadducees and the philosophy of Mr. Epicurus does not give man much hope. They are telling men that there's nothing better than this. But Man needs the hope of a better situation because this situation now is dismal, gloomy, grim, and bleak. You can't get much hope when you look around and you are besieged by trouble. There's not much hope when you look around, and you are besieged by trouble. There's not much hope in sorrows, trials, tribulations, burdens, persecution, prosecution, cares, woes, peril, pain, despair, and affliction. There's not much hope in traps and ditches, tear-stained eyes, mournful cries, broken hearts, dreary days, sleepless nights, giving up the right for the wrong. You can't find much hope in suffering, criticism, and world hatred. There's not much hope when you see funerals, morticians, caskets, and hurst wheels rolling.

The Sadducees and Mr. Epicurus don't give us any hope. But thank God, Jesus said, "I AM the Resurrection and the Life." I came to give you the hope and the assurance that this side of the grave is not all of it. Because "I AM the Resurrection and the Life," there is a life which nothing can neither destroy nor interrupt. Because "I AM the Resurrection and the Life," if you believe in Me, when death comes, then you pass out of the land of the dying and into the land of the living. Because "I AM the Resurrection and the Life," death is a gate on the skyline. Because "I AM the Resurrection and the Life," death is not the ultimate goodbye, but the ultimate hello. Because "I AM the Resurrection and the Life," if you believe in Me, death is not the end of life, nor the extinction of being.

The story is told of an old woman who died, and at her funeral, all of the people who passed by her casket to view her remains were puzzled by what they saw. What puzzled them was not the woman's casket. It was not her pretty dress. It was not even her favorite Bible. What puzzled them was the fact that she had a fork in her right hand. Over and over as the people passed by, the Pastor could hear them asking, "What's with the fork?" During the pastor's message, the pastor told them what the fork in her right hand was all about. He said that before the woman died, she told him that she wanted to be buried with that fork in her right hand because she thought about the fact that every time they had socials and potlucks at the church, after the main course was over, somebody would inevitably say "Keep your fork, because something better is coming." I want to serve notice today that something better is coming. In fact, the best is yet to come. I don't care how good life is for you down here, keep your fork as a reminder that the best is yet to come.

I know the best is yet to come because I hear Jesus say, "Let not your hearts be troubled." I heard Paul say, "For we know that if our earthly house of the Tabernacle were dissolved, we have a building of God, a house not made with hands, eternal in the heavens." I hear John saying, "Beloved, now are we the sons of God, and it doth not yet appear what we shall be: but we know that when He shall appear, we shall be like Him; for we shall see Him as He is." I know that the best is yet to come because we are on our way to a land where there is:

A prepared city for a prepared people,
A city, that is pure gold
A city, where the walls are made of Jasper,
A city, where the gates are made of pearls,
A city, where streets are paved with gold,
A city, where the walls are 144 cubits high with 12 foundations,
A city, where there are 12 gates to the city,
A city, that is foursquare,
A city, where there is a river as clear crystal,

A city, where there is a tree bearing 12 manners of fruit,
A city, where every day will be Sunday,
A city, where God sits upon the throne,
A city, where we shall never grow old,
A city, where the people wear starry crowns, long white robes, and golden shoes.

Does that sound like a ghetto? Caesar Clark said that it is:

A city where there is:
Eternal springtime,
Where glory dwells,
Where joy flows like a river,
Where peace abides,
Where dawns are forgotten,
Where nights are unknown.

My daddy said, "It is a city of no mores."

No more sorrow.
No more sickness.
No more tears to shed.

6

"I AM the Way, the Truth, and the Life"

John 14:6 (KJV) - *⁶Jesus saith unto him, "I am the way, the truth, and the life: no man cometh unto the Father, but by me."*

Everybody who is present when Jesus makes this statement is troubled, including Jesus, for John 13:21 says, "When Jesus has thus said, He was troubled in Spirit." Jesus was troubled in Spirit because of the fact that Judas would betray His love and friendship. Jesus was troubled because Judas was so spiritually hard that he would not repent. But on the other hand, His disciples were exceedingly troubled because Jesus had just announced that He was going to leave them.

In scriptural retrospect, you will discover that six months prior to the Text, in times when He had private sessions with His disciples, Jesus made repeated statements about His coming, sufferings, and death. But now, it was actually dawning on them that He was, in fact, going to die. This realization sent them into a state of bewilderment and turmoil.

They were in turmoil because Jesus was their very life. They left their homes, their families, and their various occupations to follow Him, and now, He's going to leave them. Here, He who woke up like a man, and spoke up like God and stilled troubled waters with three words, "Peace be still"; He who turned water into wine between pour in and pour out; He who fed a multitude of 5000 men (besides women and children) with two fish and five barley loaves of bread between breaking and distributing; He who cured a woman's issue of blood between touch and tell; He who restored man's withered hand between an awful command and an astonishing expectation; He who between irritation and irrigation made a blind man see; He who between the already and the not yet rebuked and cast out the Devil in the lunatic son; and He who taught them how to pray and had the cure for unbelief, has announced that He was going to leave them.

As the disciples were pondering what they would do in His absence and who would fill the void that He would leave in their aching and anxious hearts, Jesus told them something else that would add to their troubled hearts. He tells them that one of the 12 would betray Him. Then He says that Peter would utterly deny Him three times before morning.

In the midst of this troublesome situation, the disciples began asking questions. Peter asked two questions, Thomas asked one question, Philip asked one question, and Judas, who I called Jude, asked one question. Our Text is Jesus' response to the "B" part of Thomas' inquiry. Thomas said to Jesus, "Lord, we know not wither thou goest; and how can we know the way?" And Jesus answered Thomas' question by saying, "I AM the Way, the Truth, and the Life: no man cometh unto the Father but by Me."

From a grammatical standpoint, take note of the fact that Jesus takes and uses the incommunicable name "I AM," and links it with three predicates, "Way," "Truth" and "Life," but precedes each predicate with the definite article "the," thus, making the subject and the predicates both identical and interchangeable. Because "the Way" is figurative, Jesus adds two literal terms, "the Truth" and "the Life" in order to define "the Way." What Jesus seeks to get across is the fact that He is not merely a way, but He is exclusively the only straight way. He is not merely honest and truthful, but He is the embodiment, the infallible, and the sovereign Truth. And then, He is not saying that He is alive, but He is stating that He is the true, blessed, and uncreated life. He is the origin and source of life. When you examine this self-affirmation of Jesus, you will see that Jesus is dealing with the three greatest issues of the human heart, and they are: (1) reconciliation; (2) illumination; and (3) regeneration.

In order to get the right handle on this, there is something that we must understand. Before sin entered the world, Adam and Eve enjoyed a threefold privilege in relationship to God. First of all, they enjoyed the privilege of communion with God. Secondly, they had the privilege of knowing God and receiving the Truth from Him. Finally, they had the privilege of possessing spiritual Life. However, when they disobeyed God by partaking of the forbidden tree and fell into the state of sin, they lost the privileges they enjoyed. Instead of them enjoying the privilege of communing with God, they now experienced alienation from God. Instead of them receiving the Truth that flowed from the lips of the God of Truth, they fell into falsehood and error. Instead of them possessing spiritual Life, they were both dead and dying.

So, because of what Adam did, and because Adam is the federal head of man, all of mankind became alienated from God, ignorant of the Truth, and condemned to spiritual and physical death. Because of the fact that man is in a state of fallenness, every man is born a sinner, and every sinner has a threefold need; reconciliation, illumination, and regeneration. When Jesus makes His claim, He is saying that our threefold needs are perfectly met in Him. When Jesus says "I AM the Way, the Truth, and the Life," He is saying soteriologically to fallen man, that He is the answer to our grave dilemma and our central problem.

I. Reconciliation

First of all, Jesus says, "I AM the Way," that is reconciliation. When you mention the idea of a way, you are basically talking about a path to get from one point to another point. So, when Jesus says, "I AM the Way," He is saying that He is the path that leads from one point to another. Now, He is the path that leads from man's ruined, depraved existence to God the Father.

You see, when Adam fell in the Garden (of Eden), there was separation, estrangement, a gap, alienation, a gulf, a chasm that existed between God and man. Now, in order to successfully deal with this separation and alienation, there was a need to successfully deal with that which was permitted to wedge between God and Man, thus bringing about the separation. Wedged in between God and Man, thus, bringing on the chasm, was sin. So, in order to deal with the alienation problem, some very complicated matters had to be sorted out.

1. The wrath of God had to be averted, quenched, and turned aside.
2. God's wrath had to be placated so that His love could go out to embrace and save sinners.
3. Retributive justice and redeeming love had to join hands.
4. There was a need for a strange love affair and a rare romance, for mercy and *Truth* had to meet and righteousness and peace had to kiss.
5. The Judgment Seat (of Christ) had to be transformed or metamorphosized into a Mercy Seat.
6. Sin is indebtedness, and only the death of the sinner could pay the bill.

And Jesus was the only one who could deal acceptably and propitiously with these complicated matters that dealt with the sin issue. Take note of what Jesus did not say. He did not say, "I AM *a* way," but He said, "I AM *the* Way." The term *way* is not pluralized, which means, there is only one Way. There is only one narrow path that leads from Man's ruined condition to God, and that one narrow path is a person, and the person's name is Jesus.

When you examine the Old Testament, look at Noah's Ark; there was one door, and it was on the side of the Ark. Look further, and you will see that Jacob had a dream about a ladder reaching from Earth to Glory, and he saw angels ascending and descending. Notice that there were no ladders, but there was one ladder, and that one ladder typifies Christ, and Christ is the only path that leads from Earth to Glory, from Man's ruined, depraved condition, to God the Father. And the reason why Jesus is the Way is because He is the only one who is able to deal with the sin problem.

Let me tell you how Jesus adequately dealt with the sin problem. He became eligible to bear our sin upon Himself by coming all the way from Heaven down and tabernacled 33 years in a tenement of human clay. He became our kinsman redeemer, our penal or punishment substitute. He died in our place. Because we are slaves to sin by the Fall (of Adam), by birth, and by debt, and so great is our guilt, and so deep is our fall, that no one could save Man but God. So, in reality, Jehovah, who is God the Father, paid Himself with Emmanuel, who is Jesus, God the Son, so that our Salvation could be truly free.

Take note that In Genesis 3, God killed an animal to cover Adam and Eve. According to Genesis 22 and Romans 3, neither the Romans nor the Jews killed Jesus; it was God (who killed Jesus). Revelation 13:8 says that there was a Lamb slain from the foundation of the world. What this killing really affirms is the fact that God, in its realist sense, is an amateur. We know that an amateur is defined as one who is a novice—one who is less than professional. However, the word amateur is a Latin word that originally meant "someone who does something because they love it, as opposed to doing a job because they have to." God didn't have to kill Jesus, but Jesus said, "For God so loved the world that He gave His only Begotten Son, that whosoever believeth in Him should not perish but have everlasting life."

God's just wrath for sin was publicly poured out on Jesus. Jesus became the recipient of our punishment and just due. Because of Jesus' substitute, ransoming death, the guilt and the punishment of sin have been successfully consummated. The prophet Isaiah puts it like this. He says, "He was wounded for our transgressions, He was bruised for our iniquities: the chastisement of our peace was upon Him, and with His stripes we are healed." Jesus dealt with the sin issue. To show you that He has successfully dealt with the sin issue, death (which is sin's sting) no longer has a sting, and the grave no longer has its victory. Because of love, God is now free to be Just and Justifier, and to condemn sin and forgive sinners, because, in love, He successfully dealt with the sin issue. To show you that He has dealt successfully with the sin issue, look at what happens to confessed sins:

There is a story about a young theologian who used to talk to an old Christian woman regularly. Every time they would talk, the old woman would say in broken vernacular, "I talks to God, and God talks to me." The young theologian would respond by saying, "You talks to God, and God talks to you?" The old lady would say, "Yes, I talks to God, and God talks to me." One day, the young man said, "The next time you talks to God, ask God what was my last sin, and if God tells you what my last sin was, then I'll know that you talks to God, and God talks to you." Sometime later, they met and immediately the young man asked, "Do you still talks to God, and God talks to you?" She said, "Yes, I still talks to God, and God still talks to me." He said, "Do you remember our agreement?" She said, "Yes, I was to ask God about what your last sin was." He said, "Did you ask Him?" She said, "Yes." He said, "What did God say?" She said, "God said, because you confessed it, He forgot it."

The Bible affirms it, for it says that our confessed sins are: Blotted out, cleansed, forgiven, cast behind God's back, cast into the depths of the sea, covered up, forgotten, remembered no more, made like wool and snow, purged away, washed away, put away, and removed away from you as far as the East is from the West.

Because of what God did in Jesus, God has a divine "forgettery" and holy amnesia. To show you that He has dealt successfully with the sin issue, every believer in Jesus can now die to the state of sin and be raised as a new creation in Christ Jesus. To show you that He has dealt successfully with sin, we don't have to die captives in bondage under the reign of sin. To show you that He has successfully dealt with sin, we can now sing, "What can wash away my sin? Nothing but the blood of Jesus. What can make me whole again? Nothing but the blood of Jesus."

And because Jesus has dealt successfully with sin, Jesus (Jacob's ladder and our bridge) takes the believer by the hand and introduces him to His Father, and joins his hand to God's hand. And when you are joined to God's hand, that means reconciliation has taken place. And being reconciled to God means that He's not just your God, but He is your Father. That means, you are a part of the universal royal family of God. I have to testify and tell you that Jesus introduced me to His Father and joined my hand with God's hand. I can tell you that I'm a child of the King.

II. Illumination

But secondly, He says, "I AM the Truth," this is illumination. Ever since Adam believed the lie the Devil told, Man has been groping in ignorance and error. Ever since Adam was convinced by the father of lies that the God of Truth was lying, Man has had real difficulty in dealing with Truth. Sin has perverted, corrupted, and distorted our thinking and reasoning faculties. The Bible teaches that our mind is blind and reprobate. Our conscience is seared. Our hearts are stony and desperately wicked. Our thoughts are vain. Our understanding is darkened, and because of the fact that our thinking and reasoning faculties are warped, twisted, depraved, and ruined, Truth is now disported. It is now distorted not because there is something wrong with Truth, but because there is something radically wrong with us.

As a result, we have a real problem recognizing Truth. We are so messed up that it seems that we are in a kind of bondage whereby we have a perennial inclination to believe a lie and disbelieve the Truth. We are so callous in our reasoning, that lies need no evidence, yet Truth needs proof to be believed.

Like Pilate, we raise the question, "What is Truth?" But when Truth shows up, like the ancient Jews, we reject it. Somehow, we have been led to believe that Truth is found in a system of philosophies. We believe that Truth is an abstract system of integrated propositions. We believe that Truth is an impersonal ethic contained in many rules.

It is interesting that man mastered the sciences, is acquainted with ancient and modern world history, is well versed in myriads of languages, has conquered the air, annihilated distance, floats on the sea, prolongs life, and yet, is ignorant of real Truth.

I have come to serve notice that in our search for Truth, we are looking in the wrong place. We must understand that in its truest sense, Truth is really not a system of philosophies. Truth is not legal rigidity. Truth is not incomprehensible abstractions. Truth is really not found in books. In fact, Truth is not even a *what*. But in its realest sense, Truth is a *who*, and the who of Truth in its realest sense is Jesus. For Jesus said, "I AM the Truth." The carnal-minded man says that for Jesus to say "I AM the Truth" is arrogant and offensive.

But I will suggest that it is not offensive arrogance. It is the Truth, Jesus is exclusive, dogmatic, eternal, and absolute Truth.

Take note of the fact that Jesus does not say, "I tell you the truth," He does not say, "I have taught you the truth." He does not say, *"I am truthful,"* He does not say, *"I am of the truth."* He does not even say *"I am devoted to truth."* But He says, **"I AM the Truth."** In effect, Jesus is both the embodiment and realization of Truth.

In a very real sense, Jesus is Truth in street clothes.

Truth is ensphered or hidden in Him. To know Christ is to know the Truth and if you love the Truth, you will be inevitably attracted to Jesus Christ. For Jesus is the Truth.

I think I ought to tell you that no man can come to the Father without knowing about the indubitable Truth about Jesus. The Truth about Him is that He was born of a virgin. He gave the blind their sight. He caused the lame to walk. He cleansed the lepers. He made the deaf to hear and the dumb to talk. He raised the dead. He preached the Gospel to the poor. He walked on raging seas. He stilled stormy waters. He spoke to boisterous winds. The winds and seas obeyed His voice. Devils were submissive to Him. He exorcised people of evil and unclean spirits.

A man is not saved because he knows the Truth about Jesus. Satan knows the Truth about Him. That's why he wanted to kill Jesus. It is not about knowing the truth about Jesus, the real issue is about knowing Jesus. Jesus said in John 8:32, "And ye shall know the truth, and the truth shall make you free." Then in verse 36, He said, "If the Son therefore shall make you free, ye shall be free indeed."

Knowing the truth is more than knowing what is true; it is more than believing certain things about Jesus; it's more than believing doctrines; it is more than intellectual assent; it's relationship, total trust, and spiritual maturity. That's why the Lord has to do us like rolls. Rolls are placed in an oven, and the more heat that they are exposed to, the more they rise.

The Lord doesn't just want us to know Him initially, theoretically, suppositionally, or hypothetically, He wants us to know Him experientially and intimately. Therefore, what He does is, He puts us in the heat so that we can rise in experience and intimacy.

In our rising, we move to *Level Three*. When I got saved, I was at *Level One*. "I heard." But after a while, I moved to *Level Two*, and "I believe." I discovered that I was like the caterpillar, God put me into a spiritual cocoon so that I could struggle, and since I've been in my spiritual cocoon, I've graduated to Level Three. I don't talk about what I heard, and what I believe. I talk about what I know.

It is said that in France, there was a man named Charles Blondin who became famous for his acrobatic skill and spectacularism. It is said that he crossed Niagara Falls on a tightrope 1,100 feet long and 160 feet above the water. On another occasion, he pushed a wheel barrel across it, and later he stopped halfway and cooked an omelet. On another occasion, he took a man across on his back, turned around, and carried the man back. After putting the man who was on his back down, Blondin looked at the crowd, and said to an onlooker, "Do you believe I could do that with you?" The man said, "Sure, I've just seen you do it." Blondin said to him, "Well, hop on, and I'll carry you across." The man said, "Not on your life." That was a belief on the intellectual level.

That's the way most of us are. Our belief is strictly intellectual, but when Jesus says, "Hop on," many who know about Him say, "Not on your life."

When you know Jesus, when He says, "Hop on," that's more than intellectual assent. That's total trust. That's wholehearted commitment. That's belief unto Salvation. When you hop on, a radical inner transformative experience will take place. When you hop on, you will be spiritually metamorphosized. When you hop on, dying and rising takes place. For you to die in your old state of sin and rise in newness of life. When you hop on, you become free *from and free to*. You become free *from* life's tyrannical masters, and they are sin, self, and Satan, and then you become free *to* serve Jesus the Christ.

But ultimately, when you hop on, you will know the Truth existentially, realistically, and experientially. And to know Jesus is to know the Truth about God because Jesus is God's self-revelation of Himself. Jesus even said, "If ye had known Me, ye should have known my Father, also." He did say, "I and my Father are One." He did say, "He that hath seen Me hath seen the Father also."

Paul the Apostle wrote that Jesus Christ is the visible image of the invincible God. You see, Man's ultimate inner longing is to really know what God is like. Jesus, who is the Truth, becomes our illumination because He reveals to us the Truth about the God and Father of Truth.

Because of Jesus, we know that God is Spirit, He's Holy, He's Loving, He's Transcendent, He's Compassionate, He is Caring, He has feelings, He has emotions, He weeps, He gets angry, He's available to all at all times, and He has time to see about us.

Our Lord, and Savior Jesus Christ is not abstract and remote, but He is personal, for He rejoices when the lost are found. He knows what we need before we ask Him, He knows our thoughts afar off. He supplies all of our needs. He knows the stands of hair on our heads. He knows our down-sittings and our uprisings, and like the three Hebrews found out, He is able.

That is what I like to call, "illumination." Hence, Jesus said, "I AM the Truth."

III. Regeneration

But finally, there is regeneration. Jesus said, "I AM the Life." The whole Bible bears witness to the fact that when Adam fell, all of us died in him. Now, we must understand that there are three kinds of death. One is physical death. That's when the body is separated from the inner man. Then, there is spiritual death, and that is separation from God because of sin. And finally, there is eternal death; and that is eternal separation from God because Man chose to remain in the state of sin. So, when we talk about death here, we are not talking about physical death or eternal death. We are talking about spiritual death, where a man in this life, is separated from God because of his existence in the state of sin.

When we talk about being dead here, we are not talking about annihilation, but we are talking about ruination and deprivation. We are talking about the fact that we don't look like God anymore.

You see, when God made Man, He made him in His own image and after His own likeness. When God made Man, he was a perfect being. When God made Man, he was sinless. Man was created a little lower than the angels, and was crowned with glory and honor.

But because of Man's voluntary act which was instigated by Satan the tempter, because Man willfully denied the divine will and elevated his will over the will of God, because man chose not to believe God's Word, and because of Man's rebellion, sin was allowed entrance into this world. At that moment, there was a forfeiting of life, thus marking the death of Man. At that moment, Man experienced alienation and separation from God. At that moment, Man didn't look like God anymore. To show you that Man didn't look like God anymore, Man is now conceived in sin and shaped in iniquity. Man is a transgressor from his mother's womb. Man is warped, twisted, misshaped, split, and splintered asunder. Man descended from essence to existence. Man traded in a life that he could not lose for a life that he could not keep. Life diminished to such a level that it was comparable to a pilgrimage, water spilled on the ground, wind, a passing cloud, a weaver shuttle, a shadow, flowers that fade away, grass that dies, green herbs that wither, a dream, sleep that is soon over, vanity, a vapor, and nothing. At that moment, man became:

Depraved in nature,
Ignorant in will,
Blind in sight,
Evil in conscience,
Deceitful in heart,
Rebellious in spirit,
Carnal in mind,
Corrupt in thought – deficient and defective in views,
Ungodly in living,
Lustful in the flesh,
Proud in disposition,
Arrogant in attitude,
Dominated by the Devil
Doomed to eternal Hell,
Subject to sickness, pain, and suffering,
Mortal, imperfect, and weak,
Cursed of God to hard labor,
Children of disobedience,
Sinners by birth and practice,
Spiritually lifeless,
Worldly,
Altogether unprofitable,
Unafraid of God,
The center and circumference of his existence,
Concerned with self-aggrandizement,
Alive to things of this world,
Dead to heavenly things,
Dead, and lost.

Man just doesn't look like God anymore, but it's deeper than we just don't look like God anymore. The real issue is that we don't look like God because God is life, and we are dead and dying.

But when Jesus says, "I AM the Life," He is saying that He is Man's emancipation from death; that's regeneration. To show you how He emancipated Man, I remember an episode of Superman:

Faster than a speeding bullet, more powerful than a locomotive, able to leap tall buildings in a single bound. There was a man in the electric chair and just as the warden was in the process of bringing down the electrocution switch, Superman burst through the walls and stuck his arm in the way, and all of the electricity that was supposed to go into the man went into Superman's arms.

When divine justice had sentenced Man to die, when we were in the chair of death, on our way to eternal damnation, and when retributive justice was pulling the lever of eternal doom, Jesus came bursting through the walls of history. And on Calvary, He stuck His arms in the way, and all of the punishment that should have gone into us went into Him. Anybody who believes this can be regenerated. And to be regenerated means to enter a new qualitative existence. That's why Paul said, "If any man be in Christ, he is a new creature; old things are passed away; behold, all things are become new." An unnamed poet wrote, that to have this qualitatively new level of existence means that if you are in Christ, you have a God who is Sovereign, over all:

A King who cannot be dethroned,
A guide who knows the way,
A refuge to whom you can fly for safety,
A life that can never be forfeited,
A relation that can never be abrogated,
A righteousness that can never be tarnished,
An acceptance that can never be questioned,
A judgment that can never be repeated,
A title that can never be clouded,
A position that can never be invalidated,

A justification that can never be reversed,
A seal that can never be violated,
A standing that can never be disputed,
An access that can never be discontinued,
A portion that can never be denied,
A possession that can never be measured,
An inheritance that can never be alienated,
A resource that can never be diminished,
A wealth that can never be depleted,
A bank that can never be closed,
An assurance that can never be disappointed,
A strength that can never be weakened,
A comfort that can never be lessened,
An attraction that can never be superseded,
A power that can never be exhausted,
A peace that can never be destroyed,
A joy that can never be suppressed,
A grace that can never be insufficient,
A love that can never be measured,
A hope that can never be disappointed,
A service that can never be unrewarded,
A resurrection that can never be hindered, and
A salvation that can never be annulled.

If you are in Christ, you have:

A new mind,
A new heart,
New views,
New affections,
New fears,
New joys,
New love,
New hatred,

New thoughts,
New directions,
A new name,
New notions,
You are a member of a new family,
A new seat in a new congregation,
A new disposition,
New information,
A new determination,
New information,
A new foundation
A new tongue,
New hands,
New feet, and
A new testimony.

I don't know about you, but I have been regenerated because I believe what He did. Jesus promised to give God's life to all who believed in Him. Jesus wants to enter Man in order to impart to him non-perishing life. When Jesus came, the Tree of Life was once again deposited in the Earth's soil. Jesus said, "I come that they might have life, and have it more abundantly." Jesus said, "I give unto them Eternal Life; and they shall never perish, neither shall any man pluck them out of My hand." Paul says in Romans 6:23, "For the wages of sin is death; but the gift of God is Eternal Life through Jesus Christ our Lord." The apostle John writes, "He that hath the Son hath Life; and he that hath not the Son of God hath not Life."

And that's how I know I have life. That's how I know I've been regenerated, for I have Christ all in my life. It happened one Wednesday evening. I heard the voice of Jesus say, "Come unto me and rest. Lay down thy weary one, lay down thy head upon My breast." I came to Jesus as I was; weary, worn, and sad. I found in Him a resting place, and He has made me glad.

I heard the voice of Jesus say, "Behold, I freely give, the living water thirsty one; stoop down and drink and live." I came to Jesus, and I drank, from that life's healing stream. My thirst was quenched, my soul revived, and now I live in Him.

I heard the voice of Jesus say, "I am this dark world's Light. Look unto Me thy morn shall rise, and all days be bright." I looked to Jesus, and I found in Him my star, my sun; so in the light of life, I'll walk till traveling days are done.

7

"I AM the True Vine"

John 15:1 (KJV) - *15 I am the True Vine, and my Father is the husbandman.*

This particular "I AM" statement of Christ is the seventh and last of the "I AM" statements of Jesus as recorded in John. The last "I AM" statement is a statement that spells the privilege and the responsibility of abiding in Him.

In the scriptures, we find three different vines. The first vine we find was the Past Vine. Before Jesus came to Earth, the whole nation of Israel was supposed to represent God to the other nations of the Earth. God had designated Israel as a "kingdom of priests and a holy nation." Stemming from Abraham, Isaac, and Jacob, Israel was regarded as the divine community, and because of this, Israel was regarded as the vine or the vineyard of God.

Over and over again in the Old Testament, we see Israel pictured as such. The first we see of this is in Psalm 80:8, as the Psalmist reflects upon God's deliverance of His people from bondage. He says, "Thou has brought 'a vine' out of Egypt." The prophet Isaiah writes, "The vineyard of the Lord of Hosts is the house of Israel." God's message to Israel through Jeremiah was, "I had planted thee a noble vine."

The vine actually became the symbol of the nation of Israel. It is recorded that during the intertestamental period, that is, the period between Malachi and Matthew, which was 400 years. During the period of the Maccabees, the emblem on the coin was the vine. One of the great glories of the Temple of Herod in Jerusalem was the great golden vine, which was exquisitely carved on the front of the Holy Place. The vine was a part of Jewish imagery. The image of the vine represented the fact that the Jews were the chosen race. It suggested that God would protect the vine and that His promises were for them alone. Instead of this thought humbling the Jews and inciting them to carry out God's purpose for them, this fact made the Jews proud, exclusive, and intolerant.

As a result, in the Old Testament, this image of Israel being a vine points to Israel's degeneration and not her fruitfulness. That's why it says the vine produced wild grapes. Instead of practicing justice, Israel practiced oppression.Instead of producing righteousness, they produced unrighteousness.They were so unjust and unrighteous that they left their victims crying in distress. God's dealing with Israel and chastisement of them did not produce lasting results. The ultimate injustice happened when God sent His only Begotten Son to the vineyard. They cast Him out and killed Him on an old rugged cross because they had slipped to a level of degeneration. Israel was a vineyard run wild. She had now turned into "a degenerate plant of a strange vine." She had become an empty vine, and because Israel became degenerate and empty, she also became the Past Vine.

The second vine in Scripture is the future vine. The second vine of the future vine is called "The Vine of the Earth." This "Vine of the Earth" is described in Revelation 14:14-20. The future vine is the Gentile world system, ripening or being readied for divine judgment.The branches of this "future Vine of the Earth" are unsaved, disbelievers. The branches of unbelievers of this "future Vine of the Earth" will depend on this world for their sustenance and satisfaction. These branches will find nothing about Christ that is fulfilling and satisfying. Because of their total rejection of Jesus and total reliance on the things of this world, the "Vine of the Earth" along with its branches will be cut down and destroyed when Jesus returns.

The third vine is the Present Vine. The Present Vine, the True Vine. The historical record of John has us to know that somewhere between the Upper Room where Jesus had partaken in that solemn meal that we call "The Lord's Supper" and the Garden of Gethsemane, where He goes to pray just before going to the Cross, Jesus made a statement which shattered the pride and complacency of the Jews. His statement canceled and erased Israel as the Present Vine and made them the Past Vine. When Jesus canceled and erased Israel as the Present Vine, He proceeded to make Himself the Present Vine.

Jesus said, "I AM the True Vine, and My Father is the husbandman." What Jesus was saying was, that it is not the nation of Israel who is the True Vine, but "I AM the True Vine." Jesus suggests that at one point in time, Israel was like a splendid vine, but now she is like a vine transplanted to the wilderness and fit for nothing but destruction. Israel was the vineyard of the Lord who was privileged to receive faithful care from the Lord, and with all of the advantages she had received, all she could show was stinking, worthless fruit. So, Jesus says, "Israel, because of your degeneration and worthlessness, you are no longer God's vine. You are the Past Vine–you have been replaced. I AM now God's Vine. In fact, 'I AM the True Vine.'"

In scripture, the word "true" is often used to describe that which is eternal, heavenly, and divine. In John 1:9, Jesus is the True Light. In John 6:32, Jesus is the True Bread. In Hebrews 8:2, Jesus is the True Tabernacle. And here in John 15, Jesus is the True Vine.

When Jesus says, "I AM the True Vine," He says, in essence, because "I AM the True Vine," I will fulfill the superlative degree and to the uttermost, all the Father desires in a vine. Because of the fact that my spiritual quality extends above the plane of the earthly and the temporal, and because my essence is both heavenly and eternal, I am the finest realization of that relationship that my Father desired between Himself and the vine. I am the perfect realization of all that God had intended Israel should be. It is through Me and all of God's purposes for Israel shall be realized–"I AM the True Vine." Israel, whereas you represent incompleteness, inadequacy, and imperfection, to the completed contract, I represent firmness, stability, trustworthiness, completeness, and perfection. "I AM the True Vine." Israel, you represent a vine planted by God to be fruitful, but you are not fruitful. And even though I AM a root out of dry ground, I bring forth fruit to My Father. Israel, you are the type and the shadow, but I AM the reality, the fulfillment, and the Great Anti-type, "I AM the True Vine."

Israel, you are God's son, but I AM God's only Begotten Son. Israel, you are the seed that will enjoy the blessing of the covenant made with Abraham, but I AM the singular seed of Abraham par excellence. Israel, you are corporately the Lord's servant, but I AM the suffering servant of Jehovah, and also the perfect servant. Israel, you were considered the vine of the Lord, but now, "I AM the True Vine." Israel, what is said of you as a nation comes true in me as a person. "I AM the True Vine."

Jesus says, "You think that just because you belong to the nation of Israel that you are a branch in the vine of God; you think that just because you are a Jew and a member of the chosen people, and because of your race, birth, and nationality that you are a branch in the vine of God." But not so. For "I AM the True Vine." Israel, you failed to produce fruit. Israel, you failed to fulfill God's purpose in world redemption. You have proven to be a false vine. But unlike you, Israel, who once was a noble vine, I AM the genuine vine that corresponds perfectly to the name. I AM the faithful and True Vine that has done the Father's will perfectly. "I AM the True Vine" of God. I represent the starting point of a new and higher religious growth. With Moses came the law, but with me comes grace and truth. "I AM the True, the Eternal, the Heavenly, and the Divine Vine." What does it mean for Jesus to say, "I AM the True Vine?" It means:

I. The Universality of Salvation

When we look in verse 2, it talks about "every branch." And then, in verse 5 it says, "He that abideth in Me, and I in Him." And verse 19 explains who the "every branch" and "He that abideth" is. For it says, "I have chosen you out of the world."

To say that Jesus is the True Vine is to say that salvation becomes universal. To say that Jesus is the True Vine is to say that the divine community spreads beyond the means of the chosen people of Israel. If Israel were the vine, then this great salvation could have been circumscribed and limited to the people of Jewish blood. But because Jesus is the True Vine, there is a totality and all-inclusiveness about salvation. There is an "us-ness" about salvation. All of us have a chance to be joined to the vine. Salvation has no boundary lines–It is for all of us. Jesus says, "Come unto Me all ye that labor and are heavy laden and I will give you rest." "And I, if I be lifted up, will draw all men unto me." The immortal words of John 3:16 are, "For God so loved the world that He gave His only Begotten Son that whosoever believeth in Him should not perish, but have Everlasting Life."

Jesus commanded His disciples that they were to go and tarry in Jerusalem until they received power from the Holy Ghost because they were to be His witnesses in Jerusalem, all Judea, in Samaria, and unto the uttermost part of the earth. This salvation does not concern itself with Jews and Greeks, bond nor free, male or female. But this salvation concerns itself with "any man" and the "whosoever wills." The Lord wills all men to be saved. Salvation is provided for all of us in the world. Jesus did not discard a garment of glory and put on a robe of humanity just to save a few. Jesus left the battlements above, where He was the Prince of Glory "to seek and to save that which was lost." Jesus offers every man freedom from the past with all its failures. He offers man victory in the present from sin's tyranny, He offers Man the hope of escape from sin's full reward in Hell, and eternally in the Lake of Fire. He has provided for every man a means of escape from the gloom and despair of sin.

There are many who shall neglect and even reject the offer, but irrespective of that, God's salvation is for us all. Seeing how sin, with its disastrous power, had damaged and defaced us, Jesus in John 10:10, had this to say to broken us: "I am come that they might have life, and that they might have it more abundantly." Jesus said in Matthew 16:24,

"If any man will come after Me, let him deny himself, and take up his cross, and follow Me." In Revelation 22:17, it reads, "And whosoever will let him take the Water of Life freely." Salvation is for all, and it is free for all. That's why we can sing, "Free to all a healing stream flows from Calvary's mountain."

II. The Uselessness of Separation

Secondly, since Jesus is the vine, in verse 5, He also says, "Without Me ye can do nothing." The vine does and must do everything for the branches. It is the vine that draws the sap from the kindly earth. It is the vine that passes the sap to the needy branches. It is the vine that enables the branches to hold on. Branches bear fruit only by virtue of the life they receive from the vine. Branches silently receive all of the living essence of the flowing sap and respond by bearing fruit. Apart from the vine, the branches are mere withering sticks, soon to be ready for the burning.

Thus, the vine wood cut away from the vine was notoriously useless. Separation from the vine meant uselessness. The branches must be attached to the vine if the branches are to receive the life of the vine. There must be a union between the vine and the branches, for the vine is the source and sustenance of life for the branches. As a result, branches detached and apart from the vine have no life. When branches have no life, that means that the branches are useless, and uselessness is an invitation to destruction. Jesus is saying, that apart from Him, there is no life, no source, and no sustenance. Thus, there is no usefulness. In other words, there is no such thing as a freelance Christian. Anybody who is a Christian, in the Biblical sense, is not detached and independent of the Vine. There must be union and connectedness to the Vine.

Of course, because of our carnality, we have difficulty believing and accepting this Biblical axiom. Without Him, we can do nothing. Man majors in operating independently of Jesus. In a real sense, when we view sin, and the originator of sin (who is the Fevil), sin is ultimately about self-autonomy. Sin is about being independent agents. Sin is about being free from constraints outside of itself. This is called relativism. This was expressed by Satan when he wanted to take over God's throne, as well as Adam and Eve when they wanted to be like God, to know good and evil. They wanted autonomy. And still today, we have narcissistic, selfish, autonomous hearts. We want to be independent. Like Frank Sinatra, we say, "I did it my way."

Our human nature, which is anthropomorphically arrogant and narcissistic, seeks to keep us focused on our marvelous, temporal achievements. We point to our philosophers and their marvelous systems. We point to our economists and their theories. We point to our psychological insight. We point to the sensitivity of our politicians. We point to the outstanding advances of scientists. We point to our erudition or scholarly knowledge, and we point to our computer wizardry. We try to give ourselves credit for creating things when, in fact, all we have done is discover what God created, knowing that creation is about creating something from nothing.

We are full of schemes for social betterment. Whatever problem arises, we say, "Let us get our carnal hands upon it, and with a little social, political, economic pressure, and with our computers, and with our erudite, scholarly minds, we will soon straighten it up." We are determined, without the aid of the Lord, to put this disorderly world into some kind of orderly shape. We are convinced that we have arrived and come of age. Therefore, we are seeking to transform chaos back to the cosmos. We see no need for God's help. Consequently, we thrust Him impatiently aside because we are supposedly able to do some things without Him, and because we are arrogant and narcissistic, we are now trying to live life without Him. But what we don't understand is the fact that our human advances come under the heading of common grace, and that is God's grace for all of mankind. The whole human race benefits from common grace. Common grace is the goodness of God to all of mankind.

The Bible says that it rains on the just and unjust. And even though the human race is corrupt and depraved, and we are cracked images of God, God still permissively allows human accomplishments; but all of our accomplishments are because of common grace. We are experiencing God's good will to us, and temporal tokens of His goodness and lovingkindness. And because of our ignorance of common grace, we arrogantly believe that we don't need the Lord. So, we seek to live life without Him.

Since we don't see a need for Christ, there are side effects to the rationale. The fact is that we find that we are living in the most irreligious age since the birth of Jesus. We will not find another age where religion is so slighted, and Jesus is so ignored. In fact, this is a day when men want to sue you if you even dare to call the name of Jesus. We live in a time when men and women have no godly religion and feel no need for God. Unbelief is more radical and widespread today than ever before.

Though we seek to get along without Christ, we must admit that while there has been much development, there has been little progress. Progress means getting further along the road that takes you where you want to be. Our scientific inventions enhance development but do not spell progress. This is why Man is more confused, bewildered, and frightened than ever before. We find that we are loaded down with a cornucopia of phobias. We have never heard of so many phobias or fears before. Even believers have many of these phobias. What has happened is, that there is no union between branch and vine. And because there is no union between the vine and the branch, we now have unsanctified intelligence. Hence, we resemble withering branches and dead wood. The problem is that our emphasis is on abounding and not abiding.

Our major focus is on the carnal and not the spiritual. That's why there is now religious free agency. We are looking for the abounding life and not the abiding life. So, whatever church or denomination promises abounding, that's where we go. However, Jesus is quite explicit and emphatic as He says, "Without me, ye can do nothing." If branches are to live, they must depend entirely on the vine. For it is the vine that gives nourishment, strength, vitality, and fruit to the branches. In like fashion, Jesus is saying that because He is The True Vine, He is the nourishing and sustaining source of life. He is the very food for branches. We are recipients of the quality essence of Christ's life. Jesus said, "Because I live, ye shall live also." In other words, the real abounding life is the abiding life. To prove it, in essence, Jesus says, "Without me":

> You have branches but no baring,
> You have leaves but no fruit,
> You exist, but no essence,
> You have living, but no life,
> You have pleasure but no peace,
> You have happiness but no joy,
> You have a house but no home,
> You have union, but no marriage,
> You have sex, but no love,
> You have feelings, but no fulfillment,
> You have music, but no praise,
> You have loudness, but no joyful noise,
> You have togetherness, but no communion,
> You have profession without practice, and
> You have "Churchianity" but no Christianity
> – your religion is like chewing gum, all motion and no progress.
> You have religion, but no relationship,
> You have a building, but no church,
> You have assemblage, but no fellowship,
> You have a preacher, but no Gospel,
> You have words, but no sermon,
> You have study, but no insight,
> You have declaration, but no inspiration,
> You have information, but no inspiration,
> You have mail, but no message,
> You have proclamation, but no power,
> You have conversation, but no communication,
> You have gathering, but no God,
> You have a congregation, but no Christ,
> You have a meeting, but no Holy Spirit,

You have scattering, but no penetration,
You have involvement, but no commitment,
You have rootless devotion and fruitless service,
You have full hands, but empty hearts, and
You have lip service not supported by good deeds,

This word is not just for individual believers. It is a word for the Church. Churches need to understand that without Him, we can do nothing.

Let me, parenthetically say that when we become barren and fruitless, we become useless and irrelevant. So, because we are fruitless and barren, we have no further reason to exist. The divine intent of the Husbandman, who is God, is for branches to produce fruit. God knows that the Vine, who is Jesus, is perfect. He knows that He has given us privilege and favor. He knows that He has cultivated us with the indwelling presence of the Holy Ghost. He knows that He perpetually provides us with fresh grace, new mercies, loving-kindness, immeasurable love, angelic protection, extraordinary goodness, exulting unspeakable joy, a peace that passeth all understanding, bountiful blessings, marvelous miracles, and daily loads us with benefits, supplying us with needs and "don't needs." For all of His provisions and protection, all we have to show are leaves. That's not why we have been engrafted into the True Vine. We have been engrafted so that we might produce the fruit of righteousness.

Consequently, if we are not about fruit production, there is no real need for us to exist. If we are not about fruit productivity, then we are living a wasted life. If we are living fruitless and wasted lives, we must come to grips with the fact that fruitless branches invite judgment. In addition, if we experience the judgment of fruitlessness, we must be removed because we are taking up space, using up grace, with no productivity.

Under the Geneva Conventional Law, in the Code of Conduct, if a person chooses not to do their job in war, that person can be killed on the battlefield. We are in a spiritual war, and our job is to produce fruit.

Therefore, the question is, what are we doing that would prohibit God from taking us out of here? Is there any reason why God should let us continue to live? What is it that we are doing that causes God not to remove us? Are we in danger because of our fruitlessness of being judgmentally removed?

The flip side is, "I can do all things through Christ which strengtheneth me." So, Jesus says, "Without Me, ye can do nothing."

III. The Union with the Savior

The issue is about union and communion. The one way that we can tell if there is union and communication is fruit. And where fruit is concerned, the husbandman, who is God, wants quality fruit and a quantity of fruit. That's why the vinedresser takes away and purges. He purges and takes away so that the quality keeps up with the quantity. He wants a bigger crop, but He also wants a better crop. And since He has a dual priority, He "takes away" and He "purges."

The word "purgeth" means "prune." And the word "prune" is the same word as our word "cleanse." The words "taketh away" literally means "to lift up" or "to raise higher." Let me insert this fact: no plant requires more pruning than the vine. First, the gardener removes things from the branches that will sap its vitality, strength, and fruitfulness. Then the gardener raises the branch off of the ground in order for the branch to get more sun. Because of the taking away, the cleansing, the purging, and the lifting up, or the exposure to more sun, the branches are enabled to bear fruit. Bearing fruit is the singular purpose of the husbandman and the Vine. The Vine exists for this one purpose. If there is no fruit on the branches, that means that all of the efforts of the husbandman, as well as the life, the sustenance, and the nourishment of the vine, are wasted.

We are kinfolk to the vine. We need constant pruning, and we need the *taking away* or *lifting up*. When we are saved, the old nature is not eradicated. The new nature is wedded to an already-existing old nature. In that old nature, which is akin to the Devil, we are born naturally in the flesh. We are influenced and governed by the flesh. We are naturally inspired, deceived, deluded, and corrupted by Satan. Our desires, our designs, our wills, our choices, our resolutions, and our affections reflect our kinship to him. We have the propensity to do what is sinful, and earthly. Evil habits have us fettered and chained. We are so evil, earthly, and corrupted that we are unable to help ourselves–We are beyond self-help.

Because we are utterly impotent to help ourselves, we need help from an external source. When we get saved, we bring with us our fleshly corruption. As a result, our God has to prune us to set us free from that which hinders our capacity to bear fruit. God has to de-flesh that which is akin to Satan and the First Adam's sins. The writer of Hebrews labels it, "conformity to this world."

Many of us don't like the purging, pruning, cleansing, and the lifting process because purging, cleansing, pruning, and lifting hurts. When God is purging, pruning, cleansing, and lifting us, all we focus on is God pruning and cutting on us. But I need to tell us that there is something worse than God purging, cleansing, and pruning us. God's greatest judgment on us is not purging, cleansing, pruning, cutting, or chastising us. His greatest judgment is leaving us alone and letting us have our way. Did you know that we ought to shout about God purging, pruning, cleansing, and lifting us? God's pruning is evidence that we are loved and saved and are productive. Pruning is productive. For only the productive branches are pruned. It also says that God is not looking for perfection. Solomon writes, "God chastises those He loves." He purges, cleanses, and prunes those who are united to the Vine so that the branches can bear more fruit. I don't know about you, but I'd rather God purge me, cleanse me, prune me, and chastise me than leave me alone.

I must admit that the pruning process is hurtful and painful, but it is purposeful pain. It is pain designed to purge, cleanse, and remove that which would tend to divert vital power from bearing fruit. To lift us above the earthly, the pruning process hurts, but it cleanses the soul, keeps us from evil, and keeps us from being diseased and contaminated by evil. It condemns sin, it inspires holiness, it promotes growth, and it reveals power for victory. It leaves no room for anything dead or false. The pruning is not simply spiritual surgery; pruning is not just God removing the bad. There comes a time when God will even remove what we consider most precious so that we can be best. He prunes us so that we can be more fruitful. He wants fruit, more fruit, and much fruit.

There are some questions that need answering. First of all, what does God use to purge, prune, and cleanse us? The main instrument that God uses to purge, prune, and cleanse us is the Word of God. There is purifying, cleansing, and sanctifying power in the word of God. Jesus said, "Ye are clean through the Word that I have spoken." There is cleansing power in the Word. But God, who is limitless, also uses trials and tribulations, pain, sorrow, and woes to metamorphosize us. He uses sanctified scalpels as a means of purging, pruning, and cleansing us, whereby we are more fruitful. So, don't curse God when you are being pruned. That's God cleansing you so that you can bring forth more and much fruit.

The next question is, what is fruit? Fruit is sanctification, winning others to Christ, growth in holiness and obedience, Christian giving, Christian character, good works, and services, becoming more like Jesus, spiritually behaving like Jesus, and praise that comes from our hearts and lips. Paul says in Galatians 5:22-23 that fruit is "love, joy, peace, longsuffering, gentleness, goodness, faith, meekness, and temperance." That's fruit!

The ultimate purpose of fruit is to bring glory to God. That's why Jesus said in verse 8, "Herein is my Father glorified, that ye bear much fruit." The True Vine has one singular purpose, and that is to bear fruit to the glory of God. The reason that the True Vine desires to produce fruit, more fruit, and much fruit is so the Vine Dresser, who is God the Father, might receive the honor. When fruit is yielded in the vineyard, the glory does not go to the Vine, the branches, the soil, not the fruit. The glory goes to the Vinedresser. You see, the Vine supplies its life to the branches, and the branches are to take that life and use it to bear fruit. And in bearing fruit, we bring glory to God. There is something wrong with a branch that does not want to bring glory to God. Our burning desire, as a branch, ought to be to give glory to the God who made us, saved us, sustains us, and cares for us.

The final question is, what does it mean to abide in Christ? This idea must be dealt with because the key phrase is "in Me." The words "abide" and "in Me" are used over and over and over in this passage. So, what does it mean to abide "in Christ"? One thing we are sure of is, it does not mean those who profess but do not possess. We know that it is deeper than "in religion." It's about more than being a moral, upstanding person. It's not about being a pseudo-Christian. It's not about being a Judas branch, a Cheez Whiz Christian, and a synthetic saint, that is, one who appears to be united; one who is superficially connected. It's not about spiritual propinquity. It's about nearness; at, but not *in*. It's not about one who is in the church, knowing the right church jargon, and going through religious motions.

To abide *in* the Vine means that you have been grafted into the Vine and there is only One who can graft you into the Vine and that is, God. To be grafted into the Vine means that Christ is the enabling power in our lives. It means that through His grace and power, we are enabled to live the Christian life. It means that in the midst of persecution and peril, we can stand fast through the help that Christ gives. It means that we can have wisdom and Truth through the agency of Christ; it means that we draw all of our wisdom, all of our life and all of our strength from Him. It means to depend totally upon Christ for everything, and everything apart from Him is utter helplessness. It means to invest your life in His holy purposes. It means rejecting attitudes, interests, and concepts that Christ does not share. It means receiving the quality essence of Christ's life. It means to keep all of Christ's commandments. It means persevering or continuing with Christ. It means that Christ is reproducing His life in us. In short, it means I am saved, I'm regenerated, I am justified, I am sanctified, I am glorified, and assured that I will be totally glorified.

To abide in Christ means to live a life in which Christ is the atmosphere that we breathe. Because Jesus is the Vine, to abide in the Vine means that we have a chance to experience mystical reciprocal indwelling, hypostatic union, and total chimerism. You know what that is? The bird is in the air, and the air is in the bird. The fish is in the water, and the water is in the fish. The worm is in the earth, and the earth is in the worm. The iron is in the fire, and the fire is in the iron. So, because He is the Vine, we can abide in Him, and He can abide in us. The same thought of abiding in Christ is not just confined to the Christology of Jesus, it was also the theme of the life of Paul.

Throughout the writing of Paul, we encounter the phrase, "in Christ." Every action He performed, every word He spoke, and every experience He underwent, was in Christ. Paul has us to know that the Church as a whole and every individual member is in Christ. We are blessed in Christ. We are redeemed and forgiven in Christ. Everything is centered in Christ. We have our inheritance in Christ. We are glorified in Christ. Our faith is in Christ. Our ways are in Christ. Our hope is in Christ. Our power is in Christ. We are quickened in Christ. We are created in Christ. We are made nigh in Christ. We speak in Christ. The wisdom of God is manifest in Christ. We are partakers of God's promises in Christ. We begin by being babes in Christ. We grow in Christ. We are built up in Christ. We are established in Christ. The gifts of nurture and strength are in Christ, and the Christian way is walked in Christ.

Paul went so far as to say that in Christ, "we live, we move and have our being." He said, "If any man be in Christ, he is a new creature; old things are passed away; behold, all things are become new." So, to abide in the True Vine or in Christ means that you have:

>A God who is sovereign over all,
>A king who cannot be dethroned,
>A guide who knows the way,
>A refuge to whom you can fly for safety,
>A life that can never be forfeited,
>A relationship that can never be abrogated,
>A righteousness that can never be tarnished,
>An acceptance that can never be questioned,

A judgment that can never be repealed,
A title that can never be clouded,
A position that can never be invalidated,
A justification that can never be reversed,
A seal that can never be violated,
A standing that can never be disputed,
An access that can never be discontinued,
A portion that can never be denied,
A possession that can never be measured,
An inheritance that can never be alienated,
A resource that can never be diminished,
A wealth that can never be depleted,
A bank that can never be closed,
An assurance that can never be disappointed,
A strength that can never be weakened,
A comfort that can never be lessened,
An attraction that can never be superseded,
A power that can never be exhausted,
A peace that can never be destroyed,
A joy that can never be suppressed,
A grace that can never be insufficient,
A mercy that can never be restrained,
A love that can never be measured,
A hope that can never be disappointed,
A service that can never be unrewarded,
A resurrection that can never be hindered, and
A salvation that can never be annulled.

And because I am in Christ, I walk in the newness of life; for I have:

A new nature,
A new name,
A new attitude,
A new desire,

New principles,
New rules,
New ideas,
New aims,
A new purpose,
New ends,
A new motive,
A new insight,
A new foresight,
A new outlook,
A new disposition,
A new inspirations,
A new seat in a new congregation,
New information,
A new determination, and
A new face.

I speak with a new tongue.
I run with new feet.
I stand on a new foundation.

My hope is built on nothing less than Jesus' blood and righteousness. I dare not trust the sweetest frame, but wholly lean on Jesus' name. On Christ...You do know who Christ is, don't you? Well, maybe somebody does not know. So, let me tell us who Christ is. He is "the Solid Rock on which I stand, all other ground is sinking sand." But then, I have new songs: "Amazing Grace" and "Blessed Assurance."